REEF

REEF

A SAFARI THROUGH THE CORAL WORLD

Photographs and text by

JEREMY STAFFORD-DEITSCH

SIERRA CLUB BOOKS   SAN FRANCISCO

The photograph on the half-title page shows the shapes and colours of
the reef reflected in the sinuous undersurface of the Red Sea.

The photograph opposite the title page shows a roving grouper
Plectropomus pessuliferus in the Red Sea, with a grey reef shark
Carcharhinus amblyrhynchos in the background.

The Sierra Club, founded in 1892 by John Muir, has devoted itself to
the study and protection of the earth's scenic and ecological resources –
mountains, wetlands, woodlands, wild shores and rivers, deserts and
plains. The publishing program of the Sierra Club offers books to the
public as a nonprofit educational service in the hope that they may
enlarge the public's understanding of the Club's basic concerns. The
point of view expressed in each book, however, does not necessarily
represent that of the Club. The Sierra Club has some sixty chapters
coast to coast, in Canada, Hawaii, and Alaska. For information about
how you may participate in its programs to preserve wilderness and
the quality of life, please address inquiries to Sierra Club, 730 Polk
Street, San Francisco, CA 94109.

Sierra Club Books paperback edition: 1993

10 9 8 7 6 5 4 3 2 1

Library of Congress Cataloging-in-Publication Data

Stafford-Deitsch, Jeremy
  Reef: a safari through the coral world/by Jeremy Stafford-Deitsch.
    p. om.
  Includes index.
  ISBN 0–87156–541–2
  1. Coral reef biology. 2. Coral reefs and islands – Pictorial works.
3. Coral reef fauna – Pictorial works. 4. Coral reef biology – Pictorial
works. I. Title.
QH95.B.S73   1991
574.5′2637—dc20   90–25432
                                                                       CIP

AN EDDISON · SADD EDITION

Edited, designed and produced by
Eddison Sadd Editions Limited
St Chad's Court
146B King's Cross Road
London WC1X 9DH

Phototypeset in Meridien by Ampersand Typesetting
(Bournemouth) Limited, England
Origination by Scantrans, Singapore
Printing and binding in Hong Kong
Produced by Mandarin Offset

CONTENTS

INTRODUCTION

Little fish have bigger fish
Behind their backs to bite 'em,
And big fish have bigger fish
And so ad infinitum.

Jonathan Swift (MISQUOTED)

It is morning. At dawn it poured with rain. The lush rain forest shore attests to the abundant rainfall in this remote corner of Papua New Guinea. But as the sun climbed the clouds started to vanish; the forest steamed and then glinted in glossy greens; the sea turned into combinations of blue, green and tan as it etched the contours of the deep and shallow reefs below the surface.

The excitement is palpable. The other divers are struggling into their equipment, swapping the same old jokes about sharks, battling to be the first in. For once I do not enter the race. I must wait at least another hour until the sun has climbed higher, until it can better illuminate the shapes and patterns of the reef, increase the magic of the colours so that I can take photographs. So I stand apart, check again that my camera is working, try to banish the dread that a grain of sand, a single hair or a speck of anything is lying across a waterproofing seal and waiting to flood the camera.

In an hour the divers return, clambering back onto the boat in their cumbersome equipment. Some laugh and babble, joke about some timid creature, exaggerate the size of a distant shark. Others seem subdued. But I know their quietness is not due to disappointment. Far from it. They are stunned. I kit up, make one last check of my camera and don my tank. Now it is my turn.

Coral reefs are the most beautiful and fascinating habitats on the planet. It is tragic that only a small minority of the population has had the opportunity to see a healthy reef firsthand, a tragedy vastly compounded as reefs crumble and vanish as the result of environmental degradation and destruction. For coral reefs are the most brittle of victims. The scale of destruction is one consideration; the intricacies of what is being destroyed is another. Perhaps this book will help to shed some light on both.

The coral reef is an outpost for the imagination and here Nature is at her most baroque. The coral is her stucco, her palette is the iridescent splendour of the reef fish. But occasional glimpses of bulky shadows in the blue background are more ominous to the diver. The plunging dance of sunlight illuminates stately hunters, masters of naked efficiency: a shuddering tuna streaks past glittering like polished steel; a silver fog crystalizes into a phalanx of barracuda; a blur of bronze reveals the slingshot quickness of a shark. One such sight and reality immediately

A hogfish *Bodianus diana* swoops past a coral rock long overgrown by soft corals and sea fans on a reef beyond the shores of Papua New Guinea. On first exploring a coral reef the novice diver is likely to be completely dazzled, with reactions veering between bewilderment and incredulity. Although other natural habitats can approximate the sensations of remoteness and alienation that the adventurer experiences on the reef, few can reward his exploration with such a cornucopia of life. The reef seems to be a natural corner of the impossible. But as the diver gains insight into its inhabitants and workings, so he begins to appreciate the intricacies of what he is seeing.

The splendid colours of many coral reef fish are so startling that it is often difficult to imagine how they have evolved to the benefit of their bearers. Here, a queen angelfish *Holacanthus ciliaris* cruises on a Bahamian reef. Reflective guanine crystals are contained within its scales, so on a shallow, sunlit reef, a queen angelfish will appear a noble combination of blues and yellows. Then, as it turns, the sun will strike at the critical angle and the whole body will flash with a spectral iridescence. The degree of the effect seems to vary from one fish to another but young adults are often the most dazzling.

asserts itself. The reef is just another habitat governed by the same unpitying laws of survival.

A few months ago I was diving one of the most remarkable coral reefs I know – the Sanganeb atoll in the Sudanese Red Sea. I had just run out of film. Normally I would return immediately to the boat to reload and prepare for the next dive; I was there to take pictures after all, not to admire the scenery. But then a thought suddenly struck me: lugging cameras along on a dive completely alters one's perception of the reef. Some aspects are enhanced as the photographer learns to move slowly and to take in the finer details of the surroundings; though divers unlucky enough to be paired with underwater photographers insist they never move anywhere at all. But the photographer tends to see everything merely in terms of its potential to make a decent photograph. I realized that, after years of photography, something else had been numbed in me: the capacity for wonder, the sense of nervous freshness I had felt as a beginner. So, rather than return immediately to the boat, I snorkelled along the unremitting magnificence of the reef wall. Now that my camera was useless I could forget about trying to reduce everything to photographs. I could enjoy interactions that could never be captured on film, aesthetically outrageous juxtapositions of coloration that were somehow perfect. I could sense the unending tension between hovering predators and browsing prey, the hair-trigger difference between tranquillity and panic. At this level of interaction the mind, overwhelmed by the rococo extravagances of the reef, responds with awe. When I tell people about my fascination for coral reefs it is at this stage that their eyes glaze over and they try to change the subject. I wish it were possible magically to transport my audience down to a reef to see firsthand what I am trying to convey – and so I could stop ruining my dives by concentrating on taking photographs all the time.

Every underwater photograph is more or less a failure. The better the photograph, the more obvious are its shortcomings. Once the underwater photographer has mastered the technicalities of focus and exposure, the farce of composition begins. Even the clearest water is hazy and the photographer must get within a metre or so of the subject to capture a sharp image. Static subjects are not the problem; but a free-swimming fish – suspicious, shy or just plain terrified of the one-eyed, bubble-belching, underwater Frankenstein that is a diver – rarely allows you anywhere near. When you do get lucky it is normally only to record the tail-end of a fleeing fish. Robert Halstead, an underwater photographer who has dedicated his life to recording the splendours of Papua New Guinea, insists the secret is to talk telepathically to fish, to explain what you want them to do. In this way, or so he claims, they will obey you. I dispute this. I have sworn telepathically at fish and beamed the most disgraceful threats to them if they do not remain in place. They flee even faster.

The gap between what the photographer thinks has been captured on film and what the photograph actually records is often vast. This is painfully obvious to anyone who has fumbled with a camera underwater. The difference between what your imagination expects and what the processing laboratory returns is so considerable that disappointed and disillusioned beginners tend to accuse the laboratory of incompetent processing. In extreme cases – where the photographs look like surreal studies of coal-faces and avalanches – they have been known to accuse the laboratory of returning someone else's film. Yet even the best photograph is no more than a distant echo. Nevertheless, underwater

photography builds character: stoicism when the camera floods, fatalism when the flash-gun dies, resignation when the world's friendliest manta ray poses before you while your camera is set for close-up photographs.

You can always identify the serious underwater photographer on a dive boat as the one with the poker face who rarely smiles. Yet etched into that outer mask are disturbing lines that suggest this person has the capability of breaking into bouts of dangerous euphoria, the results of occasional successful photographs. To this photographer these rare successes are evidence of matchless skill; peers claim, however, that they are glorified flukes. Underwater photographers are a cynical bunch.

There are two accolades to which the underwater photographer aspires. The first is the accusation that the shots were taken not in the wild, but in an aquarium. The second is the allegation that the photographs were faked, perhaps by superimposing one subject onto another scene. I do not mean to suggest that all underwater photographers are above cheating. There is a photograph that is happily being reproduced in various publications that purports to show a large shark confronting a diver. In fact, the photographer has admitted to me that the 'shark' is a plastic model. Even worse is a technique that is rumoured to be used occasionally: squirting drugs into the water to sedate and slow down the fish.

How, then, can photographs be taken underwater without resorting to these kinds of disgraceful techniques? The first consideration is the equipment that the diver is using. A full-time professional may use several different underwater camera systems, each appropriate to a certain kind of subject. An amateur on holiday may well be using something far cheaper, simpler and more limited in its range of application. Professionals, however, do have a few secrets which I will now reveal.

The greatest gift is persistence. If you want to get a picture of a fish then be willing to sacrifice at least a whole dive and a whole roll of film to it. While on a dive a short time ago I saw someone taking a photograph of an angelfish. I could tell from the angle between the camera and the fish that the shot would not be successful. Back on the boat the diver asked me what I had been assiduously pursuing all through the dive. When I told him it was angelfish, he happily informed me that he had got a good shot of one. I remained silent. I did not want to break his heart.

The greatest skill is trial and error. The only way to gain a reasonable understanding of the sort of shots that succeed is to take a considerable number of photographs. Vary the composition, the setting and the angle of the subjects. When you get your film back study the best results and work out why they are so, but it is just as important to study the failures and work out why they did not succeed. In this way you will learn that underwater photography, like every other kind, is about recognizing which category of shot is appropriate at any one time. Do you want a full frame shot of a certain fish that would be useful for species identification but not much else? Or do you want to photograph the same fish set against a picturesque background? Or perhaps the fish should be a relatively small constituent of the photograph – large enough to be of interest, but not to dominate or detract from other features of the picture.

To achieve a successful underwater photograph, it is generally necessary to photograph the same subject repeatedly. Flukes apart, this is the way to finish a dive trip with a backbone of presentable pictures.

In many parts of the world Humankind lives in balance with its environment. Coral reefs and their surrounding waters provide a rich harvest for many coastal and island peoples. The reefs of the Milne Bay Province of Papua New Guinea have supported village communities for thousands of years and the reefs themselves are prolific and healthy. I photographed this individual (*above*) as he paddled his dug-out canoe back towards his village. In the hollow trunk of his boat was a small pile of reef fish he had caught. The extravagant intensity of their colours had already faded. The reef immediately beneath the canoe (*opposite*) is well capable of providing for the modest requirements of the local village fishermen. Communities dependent on their reefs for food are instinctively protective of them; it is the outsiders and their methods that spell doom.

This is not quite the same as the art of persistence. The point here is that if you find a co-operative subject it pays to take numerous photographs of it and vary the exposure and composition. If the subject lingers, try to set up more interesting shots of it. At the end of the day you should have a few 'special' shots.

Try to forget about photographs you think may be successful once they have been taken. Redouble your efforts to get other shots and in this way you may get a few that outweigh the disappointments. Do not look forward to getting your film processed as the pain always outweighs the pleasure.

The final secret of professional underwater photographers is perhaps the most important. They may have more good shots than amateurs, but they will almost certainly have far more bad shots. Their secret is never to show them to anyone.

The majesty that the eye sees is often recorded as chaos by the camera. In attempting to capture an underwater scene the photographer must attend to the simplest, broadest brush strokes. Fish of different species side by side on the reef provide a wonderful sight. On a photograph, however, they usually clash. The beginner will also realize before long that water absorbs colour: the deeper you dive, the less colour is visible. Cut yourself at a depth of 30 metres (100 feet) and you will see green blood. By 50 metres (165 feet) everything is blue-grey. This is why a photographer must use underwater flash-guns, known as strobes, to restore the colour balance.

Philosophical questions arise. Those colours that the strobe replaces do not naturally occur at depth, so the polychrome splendour that the camera records is in fact a ghostly potential made real by the flash-gun's burst of artificial light. This parallels the strange world of quantum physics. If it makes no sense to talk about a particle until it has been observed, then it makes no sense to talk about this world of colours until a flash-gun or torch has lit it. Presumably the answer lies in the shallows where the colours are naturally present. Any evolutionary advantage gained by coloration in the shallows will vanish at depth, but species may well survive thanks not only to that advantage. Patterns, brightness and contrast will remain valuable for camouflage purposes at depth, even if the colours themselves have gone.

But there are other, more subjective mysteries. I was once diving a spectacular point on a reef in the Red Sea. Swimming down along the coral wall to a depth of about 20 metres (65 feet) I felt as though the beautiful colours of the coral shallows were keeping me company. As I swam deeper out along the point to 30 and 40 metres (100 and 130 feet), I noted that it had become a little darker, but my eyes soon adapted. The brilliant clouds of tiny orange fish that festoon Red Sea coral heads seemed every bit as intensely orange at depth as they were in the shallows. The 2.75-metre (9-foot) silvertip shark that glided up to me for a cursory inspection had a platinum hue to her skin. I seized the opportunity of capturing this fleeting scene and took two photographs in rapid succession. In the first the strobe fired and painted the shark and the setting with light. In the second I released the shutter too soon, before the strobe had had a chance to recharge and it failed to fire. When I went to the processing laboratory to collect the film I should have been forewarned by the expression of the girl behind the counter who handed it back. She had that pitying 'You must be an underwater photographer' look that underwater photographers dread. Swallowing my pride, I examined the slides there and then. The first picture – when the strobe had fired – was just about adequate and I could just about make out the colours. The second, however, was hopelessly gloomy and dull. Yet on the dive I remembered the vivid sparks of orange of the tiny fish, the metal sheen of the shark. Here was proof that those colours had not in fact been there. This raises another question: if you took someone who has never seen the splendid colours of a shallow water reef and deposited them on a reef at a depth of 50 metres (165 feet) what – if any – colours would they see?

This is no idle digression. It is an attempt to show how subjectively interlocked so many aspects of the coral reef are to the human mind. The scientific aspects intertwine with the aesthetic and the raw thrill of wilderness exploration in all but the most rational or romantic of people. Whatever reason one has for justifying the conservation of the coral world – scientific or aesthetic – there is a deeper and more mysterious sense of concern which is obvious to anyone who has explored this underwater wonderland personally. It is the idea that to see what is at stake is to know that it must be preserved simply because it is there. By analogy, if this miraculous corner of Nature can impart such an outlook, then the outlook itself deserves extension to all the threatened habitats of the natural world.

While this book aims accurately to record aspects of the natural history of the reef, I hope it also kindles a desire for conservation in those who will never have the opportunity to see a reef firsthand. Conservation is now the first priority for anyone interested in Nature. Without it there is nothing.

PART ONE

THE
NATURAL HISTORY
OF THE
REEF

Anyone who has gazed out of a small aeroplane flying over shallow, tropical waters is likely to have seen a coral reef below. Although they are among the most fragile of Nature's domains, coral reefs are distributed throughout a vast area of the world's tropical and sub-tropical waters. They range in size from the modest to the gigantic: from the small atolls unrecorded on any navigator's chart to Australia's Great Barrier Reef, the largest living structure on Earth.

Hundreds of different species of coral build reefs. Bewildering varieties of invertebrates and vertebrates live in, on, or above them. Each creature has found its own tiny or expansive domain, from the minute, transparent shrimp hiding in its host anemone to the huge tiger shark patrolling impervious to any boundary. This is a mighty ecosystem, comparable in complexity to the richest rain forest. Here I will explore the biological secrets of the coral reef and sketch the dividing line between its health and its demise.

Coral reefs are found in a band around the world situated approxi-mately between latitudes 30 degrees North and 30 degrees South. It has been estimated that there are some 600,000 square kilometres (232,000 square miles) of reef of 30 metres (100 feet) depth or less world-wide. Approximately 60 per cent of the world's reefs are found in the Indian Ocean (including the Red Sea). Some 25 per cent are estimated to occur in the Pacific Ocean, and nearly all of the remaining coral reefs are in the Caribbean.

The small marine animals that build reefs, stony corals, require warm water in order to flourish. They are found where the average sea temperature does not fall below 20°C (68°F). The reason for this critical temperature will become clear later, as will the reason why corals cannot tolerate the hottest waters, such as the shallowest sun-baked stretches of a lagoon. The depth of the water also determines whether or not stony corals will be able to establish themselves. Coral reef communities are features of shallow sea waters; stony corals thrive in clear water of 30 metres (100 feet) or less in depth, as anyone who has dived a reef slope will have seen. Once the diver has descended below the influence of low tide and wave surge, the corals are invariably at their most prolific and diverse. After 30 metres (100 feet), the variety of coral and perhaps also the quantity are in decline. By 40 metres (130 feet), stony corals may no longer dominate the underwater setting.

The difference between an Indo-Pacific reef where soft corals are in bloom and one where they are retracted is similar to that between a black-and-white and a colour photograph. Here, on Sanganeb atoll in the Sudanese Red Sea, soft corals on the reef wall bloom in the current; though they are of many hues they belong to only one or two species of *Dendronephthya*. Beyond them a shoal of orange fish *Pseudanthias squamipinnis* feeds on plankton borne by the current. These are immensely common on reefs from the Red Sea through to the western Pacific. They seem to be a particularly rich hue of orange on the Red Sea reefs.

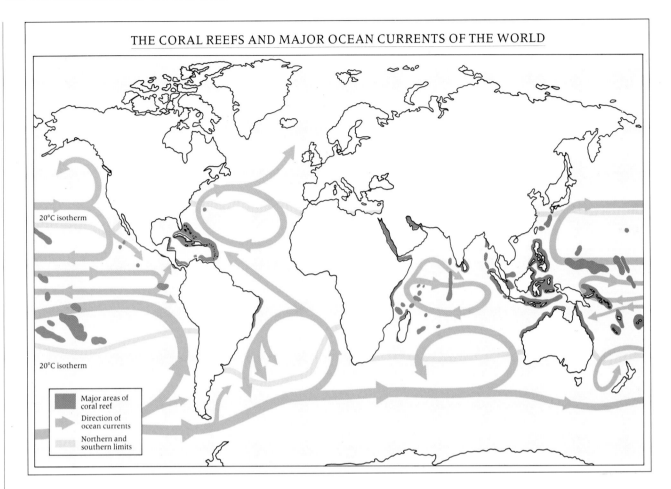

THE CORAL REEFS AND MAJOR OCEAN CURRENTS OF THE WORLD

20°C isotherm

20°C isotherm

Major areas of coral reef

Direction of ocean currents

Northern and southern limits

Stony corals lay down limestone cases that form the backbone of the reef. This coral rock allows innumerable other kinds of animal and plant to attach, burrow and settle. As one dives down to 40 metres (130 feet) and beyond, the living corals decline. The coral reef, in a sense, continues down to greater depths but is no longer a reef of living stony corals. Here the remains of stony corals of previous ages play host to a variety of life forms. When they were alive, these corals would have been found in much shallower waters, such as those in which today's living corals now thrive. A variety of factors could have accounted for their demise: the rock on which they were established could have slowly sunk to depths fatal for living corals, or a rise in the sea level could have brought about a similar result. The reef will prosper as long as new corals continue to establish themselves in shallower waters and grow upwards at a rate sufficient for them to keep pace with possible threats to their existence.

From the map shown *above* it is clear that coral reefs are particularly abundant on the eastern edges of continental land masses. Their absence from the western coasts of continents is largely due to the low temperature of the water caused by the activities of surface ocean currents. These currents are generated by the world's prevailing wind systems: the south-east trade winds in the Southern hemisphere and the north-east trade winds in the Northern hemisphere. It might be imagined that the wind pushes the sea in the same direction as the wind itself, but this is not the case with ocean currents which tend to flow at an angle of 45 degrees to the direction of the wind, due to the effect of the Earth's rotation. In the Southern hemisphere the currents flow to the left of the direction of the wind; in the Northern hemisphere they flow to the right. The surface ocean current systems of the Southern hemisphere flow in huge anti-clockwise gyrations, while those of the Northern flow clockwise. The world's great current systems hug western continental coastlines as they flow towards the equator, yet at this stage they are cold and reefs cannot flourish. As they enter tropical latitudes, the currents are warmed and both systems flow in a westerly direction. They are warm when they reach eastern continental coastlines and reefs abound. From there, the tropical currents flow away from the equator – south in the Southern hemisphere and north in the Northern – both becoming colder as they progress. By the time they return to the western continental coastlines they are very chilled.

Off the coasts of Peru and Chile, the temperature of the sea's surface can be 10°C (18°F) lower than the average for that latitude. The northerly flow of this cold water (named the Peru or Humboldt Current) makes it impossible for coral reefs to establish themselves. Further north, off the coast of Ecuador, the Peru Current flows out to sea. Its ability to stifle coral growth, however, is relatively undiminished, as is demonstrated 1,000 kilometres (620 miles) to the west of Ecuador where the Galapagos Islands straddle the equator. The waters support a staggering variety of tropical fish, marine mammals, birds, reptiles and sharks (at least before commercial fishing, particularly by the Japanese, severely reduced the protected shark population). But the waters are cold, coral growth is scant, and the volcanic rock that would provide an ideal base for coral growth plays host to other sedentary creatures.

Off the western coast of the North American continent the cold, southerly flowing Californian Current maintains an average sea water temperature that is too low for coral reef formation. Other, very different ecosystems flourish here, such as vast kelp forests.

When one looks to the waters off the eastern edge of continents, however, reefs are found in abundance. The currents that reach the eastern edges of continents in the tropical and sub-tropical realm originate in equatorial waters and provide a constant supply of warm water. Studies of the Gulf Stream in the North Atlantic show that the phenomenon of current movement is complex: huge eddy systems peel off from the main current, some to be reabsorbed, others to persist with lives of their own.

The northern limits of western Atlantic reefs are decided by the winter temperature of the sea: though there are reefs off southern Florida, none is found further north along the mainland coast of the USA. The most northerly Atlantic reefs are off the coast of Bermuda because this island group is benevolently affected by the warming influence of the Gulf Stream. Although Bermuda is not directly in its path, the Gulf Stream provides it with an enormous and constantly replenished supply of warm water. The Bermudan reefs are testimony to the stability of the system. Travel further north-east with the Gulf Stream and its temperature begins to drop below the limits tolerated by reefs. Some of the reef's inhabitants are far more hardy than the reef itself: an occasional tropical fish has been found off the British coast, for example.

There are other factors that affect the formation of coral reefs. They require saline (salty) water: corals cannot establish themselves at the brackish (slightly salty) mouths of river deltas. The water must be relatively clear as corals cannot survive in the paths of sediment carried

Continued on page 20

The animals that form the structural backbone of the reef drift as juveniles in the open water before settling and developing. The chances, however, of such a drifting creature managing to settle on a suitable part of the sea floor, and then growing and developing into part of a colony, are minute. The vast majority either perishes while adrift in the ocean, is consumed by predators, or fails to find a suitable patch on which to settle. Those animals that succeed in establishing themselves can face fierce competition from both animal and plant rivals battling over the available space. Here, in the Bahamas, an irregular area of rock has long been overgrown by such creatures. The rock provides a priceless foundation on which both animals and plants can develop. The reef structure that results when corals grow on irregularities of the sea floor is termed a patch reef. This picture was taken at the very edge of such a reef: beyond is a huge and barren expanse of sand. The current that brought the creatures here that have settled in such concentrations also provides them with planktonic food. Numerous varieties of coral, both hard and soft, can be seen as well as several species of sponge and some green mats of algae. Note the foureye butterflyfish *Chaetodon capistratus* high up in the picture. These butterflyfish typically swim in mated pairs. It is sad to see a single individual that has lost its mate.

by rivers into the sea. Off the tropical east coast of South America, for example, the vast sediment-carrying river systems of the Amazon and Orinoco effectively smother the possibility of any reefs. Similarly, off the western coast of Africa, coral reefs are absent due not only to the cold waters of the Guinea Current, but also to the heavy, sediment-carrying river systems. A recent experience brought home to me how quickly sediment can suddenly threaten to smother everything on a reef.

Last year I was diving a wonderfully rich reef off the eastern tip of Papua New Guinea. It is a small reef — about the size of a tennis court — in an unusual and precarious position, inches from a great, overhanging cliff. Stretching back as far as the eye can see is rain forest. As I was preparing to take my first photograph of the dive, everything suddenly turned dark, as if it were dusk. I knew immediately what had happened: we had been plagued by showers for the last few days and this was another. Within moments the surface was being drummed by heavy rainfall. I feared that the visibility underwater would suffer as it seemed inconceivable that the reef would not take its share of soil released from the land above. I swam to the surface and glanced at the sky, trying to decide whether to abort the dive or wait to see if things would improve. Already gashes of blue sky had appeared and the short-lived shower was moving away. I swam back down to the reef and looked along its length. A wall of silt was approaching like a dense, brown stain. It came swirling across the reef and soon enveloped everything. I could see nothing so I surfaced and returned to the boat. Looking back at the reef, the water resembled thick soup; our morning's dive had been abruptly terminated. I was initially puzzled by this occurrence. How could such a fine reef survive periodic attacks of silt? After some deliberation I concluded that such walls of silt must pay only brief visits to this reef, quickly being carried off and away by the current. This could be the only reason to explain its survival so close to the rain forest shore.

CORAL REEF TYPES

There are several broad categories of reef structure that owe their original classification to Charles Darwin. In 1842 he wrote his classic book *On the Structure and Distribution of Coral Reefs* with which the modern understanding of coral reefs begins. Darwin distinguished three main types of reef: fringing reef, barrier reef and atoll.

A fringing reef occurs close to the shore and, as its name suggests, basically follows the contours of the shore. Its stony corals require a firm base on which to establish themselves, and they have to compete with many other sedentary creatures looking for a firm substrate on which to settle. In off-shore waters, such a substrate is usually provided by the limestone secreted by previous stony corals on (often volcanic) rock. If, however, as is the case with fringing reefs, there is a firm, rocky base already present, sedentary rivals can settle in great numbers without waiting for reef-building corals to lay the foundations. Thus the stony corals need not be the major constituents of the reef. Sponges, soft corals and coralline algae, each of which will be discussed later, can be found in abundance on a fringing reef.

There are several features that determine how successfully stony corals will grow, reproduce and settle on a fringing reef. Firstly, there is the problem of low water levels. Although many secrete a protective coat of mucus as a defence against dehydration, corals die after prolonged exposure to the air. The low spring tide level acts as a barrier to coral growth. Another limiting factor, once again, is temperature. Very calm, shallow water baked by a tropical sun can get far too hot for corals to tolerate. Then there is the problem of sedimentation. Within these constraints, the reef is likely to develop by growing slowly but surely outwards, away from the shore, as new corals establish themselves on the limestone remains of old coral colonies. As this happens, an area known as the reef flat is established. This is a shallow, rocky area of dead coral between the living reef and the shore. Baked by the sun, exposed to the air at low tide, often covered in a layer of coral rubble (fragments of dead, broken-off coral) and sand, it is a highly inhospitable domain and yet one in which certain plants and animals can survive. Exactly what is found where on a reef flat varies according to the conditions. Divers staggering out across a reef flat to dive an Indo-Pacific fringing reef must wear the stoutest rubber-soled boots and shuffle their feet rather than tread: this is an area inhabited by the most venomous, infamous and inconspicuous of fish, the Indo-Pacific stonefish (genus *Synanceia*). All but invisible, stonefish have stout, dorsal spines that can inject a venom capable of killing humans.

Some of the finest fringing reefs in the world occur along the edges of the Red Sea. Here the conditions are optimal for reef growth. The water is enclosed by desert so there is virtually no rainfall to wash either sand or fresh water into the sea; and there are few clouds to affect the amount of sunlight that reaches the surface. The result is significantly warmer water than might be expected at this latitude. The reefs of the northern Red Sea are not only among the most northerly on Earth, but they are also some of the richest and most diverse. Swim over the crest (the open-water edge) of one of these fringing reefs and the first reaction may be panic: the reef drops vertically, vanishing into unknown depths. Wave action cannot stir up much sediment that would damage the reef because the sediment settles below the reach of the waves. Thus the water is clear, maximizing the amount of sunlight that reaches the reef, an important point, the significance of which will soon become clear. All in all, the fringing reefs of the Red Sea are outstanding; several of the most abundantly rich photographs in this book were taken only metres from the baking hot, lifeless Egyptian desert.

The second type of reef distinguished by Darwin is the barrier reef. It differs from the fringing reef in one significant characteristic: the area between the living coral of a fringing reef and the shore is the reef flat; but the area between the barrier reef and the shore is known as the lagoon. This is a relatively shallow area of water, only a few metres or so in depth. Some lagoons, however, can be 30 metres (100 feet) deep; yet since the foundation rock of the barrier reef is geologically identical to that of the mainland whose coast it parallels, the lagoon itself is never very deep. In terms of the depth of the oceans, even the deepest lagoon is very shallow.

The width of the lagoon can vary enormously from perhaps 100 metres (330 feet) to, in the case of Australia's Great Barrier Reef, as much as 65 kilometres (40 miles). The Great Barrier Reef actually comprises a far more complex system of reefs than originally explained in Darwin's barrier reef theory. Perhaps it is better understood as a vast combination of different types of reef (beyond a lagoon) that cumulatively form a huge barrier to the ocean.

The question arises as to why fringing reefs are close to shore while barrier reefs can be quite a distance away, separated by a sizeable, if

Continued on page 24

	LAGOON	INNER REEF
Water exchange		
Sediment transport		
Sedimentation		
Oxygen supply		
Plankton supply		
Temperature variation		
Exposure to air at low tide		
Variety of hard corals		
Variety of soft corals		
Variety of fish		

SAND

CORAL ROCK

THE REEF AND ITS COMMUNITY

This is a diagrammatic representation of an idealized reef. The reef is separated from the shore by a sizeable lagoon; hence it is a barrier reef. The reef wall plunges vertically to the immense depths of the ocean floor. After a depth of approximately 50 metres (165 feet) the stony corals of the reef diminish and then vanish. Other creatures take up station.

1. A turtle struggles up the beach to dig a nest and lay her eggs.
2. Mangroves fringe the interface of sea and land.
3. The lagoon floor is occupied by a variety of sponges.
4. A small species of inshore shark hunts in the shallows.
5. The lagoon is a favourite area for feeding stingrays.
6. Turtle grass secures the sandy bottom and slows water flow.
7. A pair of butterflyfish searches for coral polyps to eat.
8. A parrotfish feeds by scraping up algae and coral polyps.
9. Needlefish, like silver missiles, hunt just below the surface.
10. Angelfish move gracefully among the coral heads.
11. Enormous plate corals bask in the calm waters of the inner reef.
12. Battered by waves, exposed at low tide, only a few algae can survive here.
13. Ancient formations of massive coral offer shelter for feeding fish.
14. Corals are short and squat in the shallow surge zone.
15. Fragile colonies of staghorn coral grow beneath the influence of the wave surge.
16. Jacks constantly dash through teeming schools of smaller fish.
17. An ever-hungry grouper waits for a fish to wander too close.
18. Bent by the current, sea whips feed on passing plankton.
19. Soft corals swell into life when the current flows.
20. The rubble of dead coral is cemented by coralline algae.
21. Sea fans grow facing the current in order to trap as much food as possible.
22. Larger sharks tend to confine themselves to deeper water during the day.
23. Dog-tooth tunas patrol the deeper edge of the reef.
24. Hundreds of barracudas mass just beyond the reef.
25. The current has carried an oceanic jellyfish in from open water.
26. A pair of ospreys hunts the smaller fish of the reef.

REEF CREST	OUTER REEF SLOPE	DROP-OFF		OPEN OCEAN

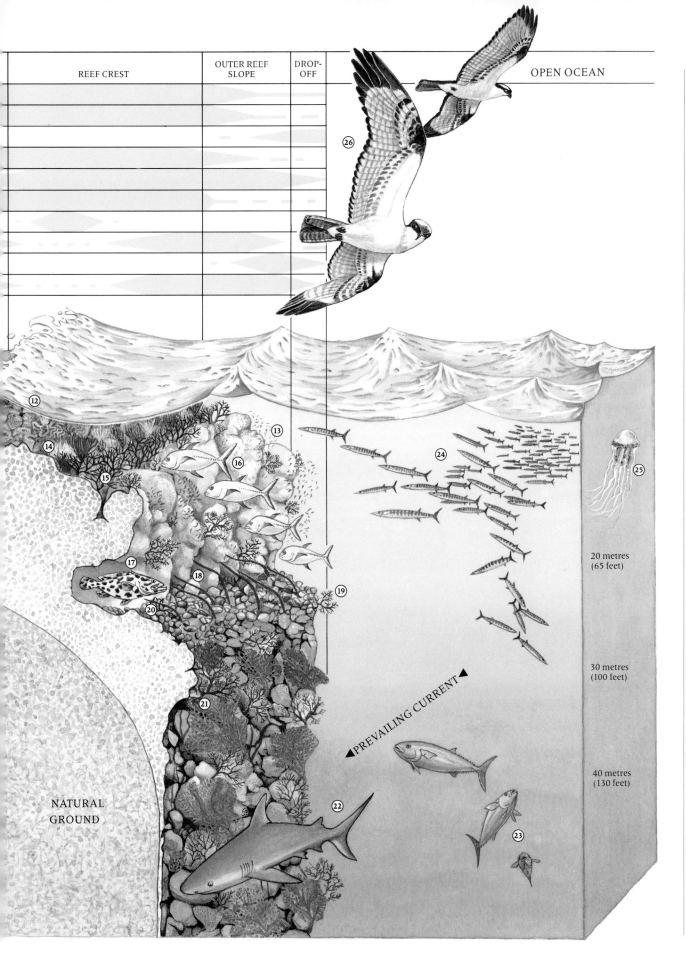

NATURAL
GROUND

PREVAILING CURRENT

20 metres
(65 feet)

30 metres
(100 feet)

40 metres
(130 feet)

shallow body of water. Darwin provided an ingenious answer. He returned to the fringing reef and asked the question: what would happen if there were a gradual subsidence of the land mass on which a fringing reef was established? The answer seemed clear: if the corals could grow fast enough then they would continue in their reef building, not only upwards towards the surface but also ever further out to sea. The extent of the latter would depend on the angle of the land mass as it submerged. If, for example, a vertical cliff submerged then it could provide foundation for upward reef growth only. On the other hand, if the land mass sank through the surface at an angle of 45 degrees, then new corals could progressively establish themselves further from shore on the area of land mass facing out to sea. The outward growth would result from the open water providing most of the food on which the corals feed. Thus the side of the reef facing the ocean would continue to flourish. The reef flat would become submerged, and the relatively barren conditions there would prevent new corals from establishing themselves. Indeed the area would become, in all likelihood, covered in the sand made from coral ground-up by wave action. In time, the distance between the reef and the shore would become ever greater, establishing the barrier reef and its sizeable lagoon. Thus for Darwin, a barrier reef originated as a fringing reef.

The barrier reef lagoon can be a fascinating place for exploration. However, given the multi-hued spectacle of a coral reef, divers all too often ignore the drab lagoon. The reason may seem obvious: it is an area mainly of sand, but there are often patches of turtle grass – a kind of seaweed – eaten, as the name suggests, by sea turtles. There are also likely to be various sorts of sedentary life. The waters of a lagoon are usually murky, the sandy bottom being constantly stirred by tide and current. This movement allows all sorts of creatures to enter the lagoon to hide, feed, mate or give birth. In fact, it takes strong nerves to explore the often sinister world of a lagoon where dark shadows frequently move past in the gloom. Anyone fascinated by the biology of the coral reef *should* venture to explore the reef lagoon. Tiny juvenile reef fish can be found here before they migrate onto the reef, and weird and wonderful creatures, invisible within or absent from the reef itself, take up station. Many fish move happily between reef and lagoon as part of their feeding cycle, so divers who explore only the reef are likely to be in for a surprise if they venture into the lagoon. Some herbivores for example, will feed in the lagoon during the day and return to the reef at dusk to seek sheltered resting places.

The lagoon is an area of unlikely encounters. I once spent a week searching the murky lagoon waters off Key Largo in Florida. On one sortie I came across an area which had been completely stirred up. I tried to convince myself that the culprit was probably just a large stingray grovelling in the sand in search of a meal, rather than an even larger shark in search of a stingray. I made a detour from the fogged-up area and continued my swim. A little later a shadow approached and materialized into a magnificent spotted eagle ray *Aetobatus narinari*. Beating its 2-metre (6½-foot) wings, it circled only a few metres away for nearly a minute before losing interest and fading back into the murky background. I have never known an eagle ray encountered on a reef to be anything but highly timid; why this individual should have behaved so differently I cannot imagine. Needless to say, my camera was set for close-up shots and I failed to photograph this magnificent creature. Shortly afterwards I saw a turtle that sped off in panic. I was

HOW A FRINGING REEF BECOMES AN ATOLL

Darwin hypothesized that the three major types of reef could be seen as stages in a process that combines reef growth with the submergence of the underlying bedrock. Although a valuable model for interpreting some reefs, other examples do not fit this scheme.

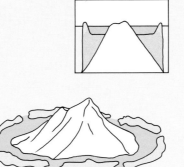

Living, growing coral

Dead coral rock

Lagoon

FRINGING REEF Volcanic activity can produce new islands that provide a shallow substrate on which fringing reefs can form. Such reefs occur in the mid-Pacific Ocean.

BARRIER REEF If the island subsequently submerges, a barrier reef can develop provided upward coral growth can keep pace with bedrock submergence.

ATOLL The culmination of the process is an atoll. Atolls formed thus are evidence of more ancient volcanic activity and are often geographically isolated.

beginning to be wary: the numerous potential meals for large predators in this area suggested the possibility of more powerful presences. When I saw the crescent tail of a shark swaying away in front of me I decided that enough was enough, for that day anyway, and returned to shore.

The third type of reef discussed by Darwin is the atoll reef, a more-or-less circular crest of coral with a central lagoon. Atoll reefs offer spectacular opportunities for diving. Usually remote, far from the influence of humans and set in deep, clear water, they include some of the best reefs on the planet. Three different atolls were dived during the photography for this book: Osprey Reef, 120 kilometres (74 miles) beyond the outer edge of Australia's Great Barrier Reef, and Sanganeb and Shaab Rumi atolls, located offshore in the Sudanese Red Sea.

There may be a few areas on an atoll reef where sand is exposed to the air. The reef acts as a trap for sand and, given occasional storms and persistent currents, banks of exposed sand and small sand islands can form. Nevertheless, an atoll exists independently of a major land mass. An atoll reef is usually only a few kilometres in diameter. To explain the formation of a coral atoll, Darwin continued the reasoning that led him from a fringing reef to a barrier reef and took it a stage further: what if a land mass – such as an oceanic island or volcano – that was encircled by a barrier reef were to gradually submerge? Provided that coral growth could keep pace with the rate of submergence, eventually a circular crest of coral would be all that was visible from above the surface.

The elegance of Darwin's argument did not convince everyone. The idea that land could indeed subside seemed, in his time, controversial at best. A rival theory known as the glacial control theory was suggested by Reginald Daly in 1919. He focused on the fall and rise in sea level during

Continued on page 28

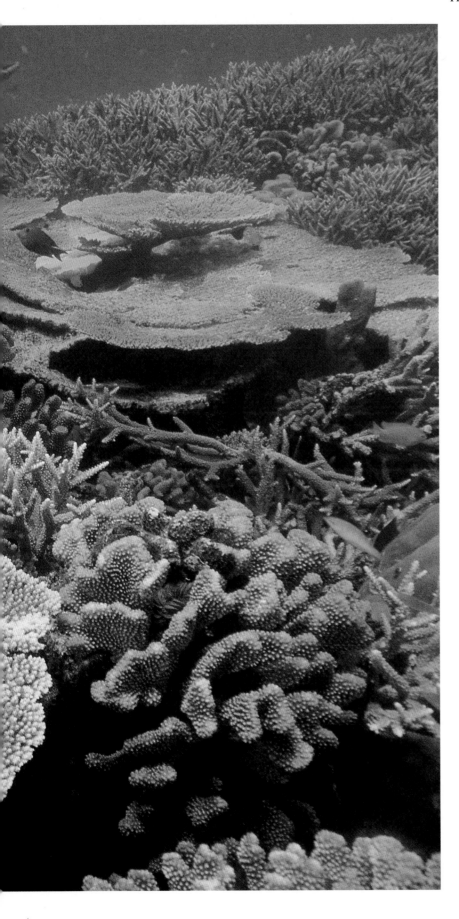

Numerous features account for the variety of life to be found on reefs, and the range of animal species that contributes to a particular reef can vary from the limited to the seemingly endless. Here, on an offshore reef in Papua New Guinea, a fine spread of hard corals is in evidence, but little else. The number of species of hard coral is small: the thickets and plates are varieties of *Acropora* and there are also a few stubby, bluntly rounded colonies of *Pocillopora*. There are few fish and no soft corals to be seen. This small reef exists in isolation in clear water far from others. The planktonic richness of currents that reach the reef is limited, thus restricting the range of other creatures that can live here. Another crucial factor is the abundance of other reefs in the immediate area. It is well known to biologists that the larger the area of habitat available, the greater the number of species that will occupy it. A large area of available reef space provides innumerable subtle variations of habitat that are reflected in a much wider range of species. When other features are constant, larger reefs in close proximity to others are therefore likely to have a much greater range of species present than small, isolated reefs.

glacial and inter-glacial periods to explain the origin of modern reefs. During an ice-age the sea level would fall because an enormous amount of water was locked up in continental ice sheets. The fall in the sea level would expose and kill coral reefs. Huge areas of shoreline, unprotected by reefs, would be eroded by the ocean. At the end of the ice-age, as the ice melted and the sea level rose, corals would grow upwards on available sites and establish the patterns of reef Darwin described, without requiring his theory of a fringing reef evolving into a barrier reef that subsequently evolves into an atoll. The site upon which the corals established themselves would thus explain the origin of the type of reef.

Today there is far more information available on the formation of reefs. The theory of plate tectonics revives Alfred Wegener's earlier theory of continental drift (1912). Wegener elaborated the idea that continents are not static monoliths but moving and changing systems whose present distribution and shapes are best understood in terms of the break up, migration and collision of earlier, radically different continents. The theory of plate tectonics links this theory with that of sea-floor spreading: volcanic material is constantly being extruded from cracks and vents in the ocean floor and spreading away from its point of origin. Given that the modern outlook suggests that the surface of the Earth is a dynamic and complex series of often gradual and sometimes violent processes, it appears likely that elements both in Darwin's and Daly's theory are valid in explaining the origins of different sorts of reef. Research tends to reveal that the processes of reef formation are considerably more complex and varied than was originally supposed.

The three terms used by Darwin to describe reefs – fringe, barrier and atoll – are not all-encompassing. Reefs have been formed in the Caribbean arising from dramatic sea-level changes caused by the last ice-age. While, like Darwin's barrier reefs, these reefs have lagoons, the width of the lagoons measures in metres and not, as in the case of Pacific reefs, in kilometres. As it is likely that these reefs originated according to Daly's, rather than Darwin's model, some authorities prefer to refer to them as bank reefs.

There are still other types of reef. Patch reefs occur in clear, shallow waters where the bottom is firm enough to support the growth of coral. They are fairly flat in profile and map the contours of the bottom. Another type of reef, called a bommie in Australia, is a small, discrete coral formation rising high above a usually sandy bottom. Such structures are often less than 20 metres (65 feet) in diameter. There are curious areas in the Coral Sea beyond the Great Barrier Reef where areas of sand seem to sprout these huge, isolated columns of coral. In some instances the top of the bommie has an impressive overhang of living coral and the structure takes on the appearance of a giant mushroom. If the sea is calm, a bommie can be all but impossible to spot from above the surface and is a considerable danger to boats.

HOW THE REEF IS BUILT

Having gained some idea of coral reefs on a colossal scale, it is time to focus attention down to the microscopic level to understand how these enormous biological systems have come into existence. After all, the Great Barrier Reef is the only living structure visible from outer space, and at 2,000 kilometres (1,240 miles) in length may well be the largest ever built on Earth. How are such natural 'goliaths' built?

Perhaps the greatest wonder of it all is that the mighty reef ecosystems owe their existence to a pact between two of the simplest life forms: one a modest animal, the other a modest plant. I will begin by sketching the details of the animal, then those of the plant and explain the remarkable association between the two. It should then be apparent why a coral reef is, in one sense, a garden of stone flowers.

The animal in question is known in zoology as a coelenterate. The term designates a group of animals that has evolved an internal body cavity lined by specialized cells. This cavity opens to the exterior by only one structure, the mouth. Simple though this basic plan is, it is an advance on even more simply designed animals such as sponges. The umbrella term (phylum) used by zoologists to name the group to which the coral animal belongs used to be the Coelenterata; for various reasons that need not concern us here, the phylum is now more commonly called the Cnidaria and their members cnidarians. I mention this in passing because the two names are both current and could cause confusion to anyone reading different texts on the subject.

Cnidarians come in a staggering variety of shapes and sizes, but the basic body plan is analogous to a double-walled balloon. Around the opening (or mouth) are found tentacles armed with specialized cells which sting, tangle or adhere to food items that are then passed into the mouth for digestion. Some cnidarians – such as jellyfish – are free-swimming, and their basic body shape is known as the medusa form. Cnidarians that build reefs, on the other hand, have a different body shape known as the polyp form where the mouth and tentacles are opposite the point of attachment. The individual animals that build a coral reef are therefore known as coral polyps. They build reefs by depositing limestone cases – known as corallites – under and around themselves. Not all coral polyps that build such cases also build reefs, however, but those that do are often referred to as stony corals or hermatypic corals of the order Scleractinia.

Why, then, when so many species of coral polyp deposit limestone, do only some manage to build the world's vast reef structures? To understand this we must move to the other participant previously mentioned – the plant. This is a tiny, single-celled alga belonging to a group known as the dinoflagellates (order Dinophyceae). The plant plankton of the sea – known as phytoplankton to distinguish it from animal or zoo-plankton – consists of mostly microscopic, single-celled plants of which the dinoflagellates are among the most common. A typical dinoflagellate has two hair-like processes known as flagellae. The transverse flagellum is contained within an open groove that runs around the plant's body and the longitudinal flagellum is projected into the water. The transverse flagellum vibrates and the longitudinal flagellum twitches and flicks. The result is that the plant is propelled through the water in a somewhat haphazard spiral. In tropical seas most varieties of dinoflagellate are found in open water and eaten by various kinds of animal. One species, however, *Symbiodinium microadriaticum* lives within the tissues of coral polyps. There are many different strains of this alga, collectively known as zooxanthellae, and they are responsible for the various subtleties of colour that healthy stony corals display. The coral polyp is transparent to maximize the amount of light that reaches its zooxanthellae.

It is the simple fact that a variety of plants live within the tissues of certain cnidarian polyp hosts that gives rise to the world's coral reefs. The arrangement is to the immense advantage of both parties. Any coral polyp that can support a culture of plant cells gains from the products of

THE NATURAL HISTORY OF THE REEF

THE ANATOMY OF A STONY CORAL POLYP AND CORALLITE

The stony coral polyp (*below left*) has been partly cut away to reveal its internal anatomy. Connected to the body cavity and radiating from the mouth of the polyp are hollow tubes known as tentacles. Captured food items are passed from the tentacles to the mouth. Zooxanthellae are contained within special sacs and distributed throughout a wide area of the polyp's tissues but tend to be concentrated in the tentacles; some can now be seen escaping from the damaged areas. Numerous outgrowths from the inner surface of the body wall partition the hollow body cavity.

The polyp secretes a limestone cup beneath and around itself called the corallite. This has numerous ridges in its wall, known as septo-costal plates. Tissue from the polyp covers and grows upwards from these plates, subdividing the body cavity. Outgrowths from

the body wall, called mesenteries, are responsible for enzyme secretion and digestion and become progressively folded towards their base. The gonads develop from mesenteric tissue.

In this simplified diagram the living tissue has been removed to show part of the underlying corallite, including a septo-costal plate and part of the corallite wall. Polyps are connected by a thin layer of tissue known as the coenosarc. Nervous connections run between polyps, hence neighbours of the damaged polyp withdraw for protection (*top right*). An empty corallite reveals its structure (*bottom right*). This includes the wall, the inner part of the septo-costal plate referred to as the septum, and the outer part, the costa. At the base of the corallite are paliform lobes to which the base or pedal disc of the polyp is attached.

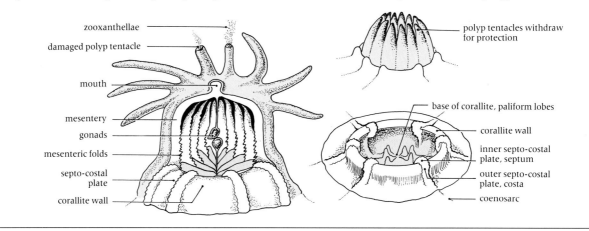

zooxanthellae
damaged polyp tentacle
mouth
mesentery
gonads
mesenteric folds
septo-costal plate
corallite wall

polyp tentacles withdraw for protection

base of corallite, paliform lobes
corallite wall
inner septo-costal plate, septum
outer septo-costal plate, costa
coenosarc

the plants' photosynthesis. This is the process whereby plants use the energy of sunlight to convert carbon dioxide and water into various sugars and oxygen. This oxygen can be used by the animal to increase its respiration. All the processes of animal life – growth, feeding, movement, sex-cell formation and so on – require energy. Respiration is the method whereby animals gain this energy. Oxygen is added to organic (carbon-based) compounds and the energy needed to fuel the life processes is released, together with carbon dioxide. Thus a coral polyp has, thanks to an extra supply of oxygen from the photosynthesis of its zooxanthellae, an added amount of one of the crucial raw materials needed to drive its life processes. Better still, the polyp has access to a steady supply of the other vital raw material it needs for respiration: it has been estimated that a coral polyp can absorb as much as 98 per cent of the organic carbon (the various sugars) produced by its plants as a by-product of photosynthesis. Again, by a complex process that is not fully understood, it seems that the photosynthetic activity of the zooxanthellae allows the coral polyp to extract rare and valuable nutrients such as nitrogen from the sea water. Indeed, in optimum conditions of water clarity and sunlight a coral polyp hardly needs to feed by the traditional cnidarian method – capturing prey with its tentacles – as plants in its tissues provide, directly and indirectly, virtually everything it needs.

30

The coral polyp therefore gains considerable benefits from possessing algal cells in its tissues. Some of the advantages for the zooxanthellae are obvious: firstly, they gain protection from the limestone case built by the polyp; secondly, the polyp's battery of stinging cells makes these algae far safer than their cousins drifting in open water; thirdly, due to the polyp's ability to actively absorb nutrients from the sea water, its algae have access to considerably higher concentrations of these raw materials than they would have if they were adrift; and finally, carbon dioxide, vital for photosynthesis, is provided as a waste product of the polyp's respiration. Biologists call such a situation – where two organisms of different species co-exist over a fairly long period of time – a symbiotic relationship. There are several forms of symbiosis: parasitism, where one organism benefits and the other is harmed; commensalism, where one benefits and the other is unharmed; and, as in this case, mutualism, where both organisms benefit.

Corals succeed in building reefs because they lay down their limestone cases in small, densely packed formations. Energy provided by the plants allows for the deposition of the backbone of the reef at a rate faster than it is eroded by the actions of the sea.

The vital yet delicate relationship between coral polyp and zooxanthellae explains why coral reefs can only exist in warm, shallow seas. Light, which is absorbed by water, is necessary for photosynthesis to occur. Because reef-building corals are dependent on their plant partners, they need shallow, sunlit waters for photosynthesis to occur most rapidly. These conditions are also essential for the successful deposition of the corallite by the coral polyp. The optimum temperature for this to take place is between 26°C and 27°C (79°F and 81°F). Once the temperature falls below 23°C (73°F) or rises above 29°C (84°F), the rate of calcification rapidly decreases and the forces of erosion overwhelm those of growth and repair. Prolonged temperature changes therefore spell doom for a reef.

Anyone diving on a reef in clear, tropical waters might well be struck by a simple thought: the clarity of the water betrays the fact that it is relatively barren with little food to be seen; yet the staggering wealth of the reef somehow exists in this underwater desert. The nutritional poverty of the water is, however, to the advantage of the zooxanthellae because its resulting transparency allows as much sunlight as possible to reach them, optimizing their photosynthetic rate.

The reef is to a large extent a self-sustaining, recycling system. Even when the stony corals do supplement their diet by feeding on zooplankton, much of it is derived from the reef itself. During the day the zooplankton is hidden under ledges, in cracks and in crevices. During the night it comes out to feed, and to be fed on, by the coral polyps.

Anyone who dives on a reef at night is likely to be struck immediately by two interconnected sights. Firstly, the coral colonies that, during the day, look like variously coloured patterns and patchworks of rock, have now assumed a softer, fuzzy appearance. Upon closer inspection the reason becomes apparent: the polyps have extended their tentacles and are feeding. As the diver gazes at the feeding corals, their food is drawn to the light emitted from his or her underwater torch like moths to a flame. Innumerable tiny creatures, absent in daylight, are wriggling and flitting about in the beam. Some of this zooplankton has ascended from greater depths, but a substantial amount is derived from the reef itself. Much will fall into the grip of polyp tentacles, but more will survive.

Continued on page 35

REEF BUILDERS AND DWELLERS

A coral grouper *Cephalopholis miniata* (1) glides across a reef off Papua New Guinea. This scene demonstrates the major structural themes that confront the explorer of a coral reef. Scale is given by the grouper which is about 20 centimetres (8 inches) in length.

A coral reef can be built by a combination of a vast variety of stony corals. Here several types are illustrated. The fact that they are set in bulbous clumps betrays the severity of currents that surge across this reef. The density of feeding creatures in the scene demonstrates the organic richness of those currents.

Off-centre (2) are two small colonies of *Porites* coral. Such corals can form great, monolithic shapes of 8 metres (26 feet) or more in height. *Porites* colonies are either male or female; the female colonies do not, like so many stony corals, release their eggs into the open water for fertilization, but rather depend on the spermatozoa from the male colonies reaching them.

Several varieties of stony coral such as *Goniastrea* and *Platygyra* form colonies commonly known as 'brain corals' (3). To identify each species, microscopic examination of the skeletal structure is often necessary.

The surfaces of some stony corals, such as the bubble corals *Physogyra* (4), are smothered by vesicles that hide the underlying polyps. This mechanism is presumably protective,

as any diver careless enough to brush against such a coral can attest: he will be stung. It is always worth examining these kinds of coral close up: many colonies have tiny, transparent shrimps resting on them.

The beautiful *Stylaster* coral (5) is far too fragile to contribute to the building of a coral reef. These corals can be found in pale varieties of pink and violet and favour the shade of ledges and overhangs. Here they do not have to compete with the sunlight-dependent stony corals.

Soft corals of the genus *Dendronephthya* (6) are one of the visual glories of Indo-Pacific reefs. Like other soft corals, their polyps have eight tentacles; stony coral polyps have six, or multiples of six. Soft corals feed by filtering organic matter from the current.

All the other major components of this photograph (7) are sponges. As can be seen, there is considerable variation in shape and coloration. Sponges are filter feeders whose basic body plan comprises numerous small pores that take in water to be filtered, and fewer large pores through which the water is expelled. Some sponges grow in a layer across coral rock. Others will bore deep into the coral to establish themselves. Identification of each species depends on microscopic examination of the small, rod-like structures, spicules, within the sponge that give support.

When diving at night I sometimes turn off my torch and let my eyes slowly adjust to the relative darkness. On my first nocturnal reef dive some years back, as my pupils dilated and the moonlight gradually lit vague shapes, I realized that another world of activity was being enacted. Creatures with eyes ten times more sensitive than mine were feeding in a kingdom which, for them, was as bright as daylight. As I gazed into the open water beyond the reef I saw a glowing, moving area. Fear pulsed through me as I wondered what kind of creature it might be. A part of me wanted to switch on my torch and boldly shine it out into the darkness but I realized that this would have only served to publicize my presence. I preferred to delude myself that I was invisible. Then, trying to identify the huge, glowing shape undulating towards me and then banking away like an enormous, slow-motion bat, I remembered the moment I first jumped into the liquid blackness at the start of the dive. For a second the water around me had seemed to burn like sparks of magnesium ignited by the violence of my entry, and someone from the boat had shouted that this was caused by the presence of phosphorescent plankton in the water. I now pushed the flat of my hand through the water in front of my face mask to prove to myself that this explanation was correct. Sure enough, a few tiny points of light glowed briefly in the surge created. I looked nervously back at the area beyond the reef that had seemed to generate its own ghostly light. I realized it must be a giant manta ray *Manta birostris* also feeding on the plankton by ploughing through the inky water with gaping mouth, now only metres away from me. I watched as it moved off along the reef, taking its flapping layer of light with it.

The manta, like any other passing predator, is a break in the recycling patterns of the reef, feeding on the reef's richness and then moving on. Recycling, however, is by no means confined to the microscopic level of the reef. It occurs throughout the food chain up to the reef's own population of resident fish predators. Provided that a plant or animal of the reef is eaten by a resident animal, its nutrient composition will remain within the ecosystem of the reef itself. Even if the animal were to die on the reef having somehow avoided the intense pressures of predation, it would be devoured by the reef's own scavenging worms and crabs.

One might think that the number of different species of animal — coral, crustacean, fish and so on — to be found on coral reefs around the world is more or less constant, but this is not the case. The greatest variety of species is to be found in the tropical waters north of Australia. The Celebes, Arafura and South China Seas and the Papuan waters of the Bismarck and Solomon Seas, to which we will be travelling during the course of this book, contain a greater wealth of species than any other marine environment. This is thought to be due to the history of the sea floor over immense periods of geological time. A glance back at prehistory will explain something of the modern situation. The corals that build reefs, the scleractinian corals, replaced earlier types of coral known as rugose corals, that disappeared 200 million years ago. It is thought that scleractinian corals originated in the shallow waters of the prehistoric Tethys Sea that has long since vanished due to the phenomenon of continental drift. However, it was in the waters north of Australia that the survivors of that sea first established themselves. Thus the peerless variety of species found here can be accounted for by the fact that these types of animal have been evolving longer in this area than in any other marine location.

This photograph was taken on a patch reef in the Bahamas. There is not much hard coral to be seen. In fact the only conspicuous hard coral colony is the lettuce-leaf coral *Agaricia agaricites* in the bottom right-hand corner of this surreal formation. No doubt the entire structure was originally a thriving colony of stony coral, perhaps boulder coral *Montastrea annularis*, but that was long ago. The formation has been almost entirely conquered by an impressive variety of sponges. Apart from the soft corals at the top and the green mats of algae on the upper surface of the left shoulder, nearly everything else is one sort of sponge or another. There is some pale red fire sponge *Tedania ignis* in the central area. At the very top, green in colour despite its common name and easily identifiable by the large pore openings for exhalation, is a lavender tube sponge *Spinosella vaginalis*. Closer inspection would reveal that it is covered in colonial anemones *Parazoanthus parasiticus*. Several more sponge species are present, including numerous long, thin, lilac-coloured tube sponges. Some sponges attach themselves to a surface (the encrusters) while others bore deep into coral (the borers). The latter can eventually destroy large areas of coral rock.

The reefs of the Caribbean evolved later than those of the Pacific and Indian Oceans as a result of the relative youth of the Atlantic Ocean. They cannot compete with their distant Indo-Pacific cousins in terms of the number of species of coral or fish. For example, consider the gorgeous butterflyfish (family Chaetodontidae), of which we will be seeing several photographs in Part Two. Five different species of butterflyfish have been recorded on the reefs of the Caribbean; yet on the reefs of the Indian and western Pacific Oceans there are about 80 species. So although you may need only a few dives on a Caribbean reef to see nearly all of the corals and fish that can be found there, on Indo-Pacific reefs several dives are needed just to realize the sheer variety of life. Of course many species of coral and fish are widespread throughout the Indo-Pacific, and some species of fish are found on both Indo-Pacific and Caribbean reefs, but others have limited ranges. Many species found on the remote reefs of Hawaii, for example, are endemic to Hawaiian reefs. The masked butterflyfish *Chaetodon semilarvatus* shown on page 97 can only be found in the Red Sea and Gulf of Aden.

CORAL SHAPES

Stony corals come in seemingly unending shapes. Some grow into huge, ponderous structures while others assume fragile forms. Some look like the petrified leaves of cabbages, others like immense thickets of tangled fingers. My mind wanders back to a reef in Kimbe Bay off Papua New Guinea. The dive operators from Walindi Plantation keep this location secret with good reason. The corals have taken on the most astonishing but fragile patterns. They have assumed magnificent flat formations that divers know as plate or table corals. Tier upon delicate tier, the plate colonies, each 2 metres (6½ feet) or more across, bask in the calm, clear water. Each is supported by a single and seemingly too-thin stem. The whole reef slope is a progression of these hanging canopies of coral and sooner or later the inevitable will happen. Perhaps it will be due to the dangling fin of a careless diver, or perhaps one of the coral stems will simply snap under the weight of its overhead canopy and a plate coral will break away and tumble down the reef slope taking the others with it like a sequence of dominoes. Little wonder that any diver lucky enough to be shown this reef must promise to hover well above the formations.

It is natural to think, as one gazes across an expanse of corals, that the unending range of shapes they assume belong to different species, and that a knowledge of shape identifies the species. In some cases this is true: the soaring architecture of Caribbean elkhorn coral *Acropora palmata* is unmistakable; and the common name perfectly describes the visual appearance of the species. But reality – and common names – rarely converge so tidily as many coral species adopt very different shapes in various locations. In shallow areas of the reef that are exposed to wave action, corals are short and squat, strong enough to survive all but the most severe of storms. Swim down into calmer depths and those same species experiment with fragility; they assume thinner or flatter forms that serve to maximize the amount of light that can reach their symbiotic algae.

The mechanisms whereby different forms are adopted are several and complex. Once an individual coral polyp settles on a suitable surface it reproduces itself by budding: replicating genetically identical versions of itself. One method of reproduction is for the original polyp to simply divide in two. Another method is for daughter polyps to grow out of, and then become established independently of, the mother polyp. In some species of coral, the method of budding adopted determines the shape of the coral colony. There are other subtle processes at work, however, that depend on the kinds of limestone wall established between each polyp. Some polyps secrete their own discrete walls, while others have interconnected walls that come in varying degrees of elongation and different patterns. Microscopic examination of these shapes is a crucial part of species identification for coral biologists.

There are other factors that can determine the shape a coral colony assumes. For instance, if a coral colony is attempting to establish itself in an already crowded area, it must either form compact shapes or battle with other corals for the limited space available. There are also genetic pre-conditions on the shapes coral colonies can adopt. Some species seem to be programmed to have a 'plastic' capacity when growing and can take on a considerable variety of shapes; others are limited to only a certain number of possible formations. The successful colony assumes the most effective structure for the conditions present.

Whichever method is used, the advantage is tremendous as corals can adapt their forms to fit different locations on the reef. Each site will vary not only in the amount of plankton and/or sediment supplied by currents, but also in the significance of wave action and the strength of sunlight. To the untrained eye gazing down a reef slope, it might appear that half a dozen different species of stony coral are in residence. But to the biologist (armed with a magnifying lens to double-check) they may all turn out to be differently shaped versions of a single species.

CORAL REPRODUCTION

One method by which a coral colony grows – the successive replication of polyps that originated with a single original parent – is an asexual form of reproduction. The genetic make-up of each daughter polyp within the colony is identical to that of the original parent. In some instances certain species of stony coral will eject a daughter polyp that is capable of settling elsewhere and producing a new colony, but this is unusual. Sexual reproduction is by far the most important method for stony corals to produce the polyps that are destined to establish new colonies.

Sexual reproduction means that half the genetic material necessary for the offspring is provided by one parent, half by the other. This method produces ever-new combinations of the genetic material and is of inestimable evolutionary value: it allows for constant mutations and hence potential adaptations to new conditions. While most stony corals are hermaphrodite – containing both male and female sex cells (gametes) – they go to considerable lengths to fertilize the sex cells from other colonies and appear to avoid fertilizing their own.

The problem here is that the stony corals are immobile: a colony can hardly set off across the reef in search of a mate. The problem is solved in one spectacular stroke. All the coral colonies of a given species on the same reef synchronize their spawning, ejecting their eggs and sperm into the water at the same time. On the Great Barrier Reef the most massive spawning occurs at night for a few days after the full moon of the late spring. As much as six months before this event, the eggs of the stony corals start to develop; the spermatozoa, on the other hand, develop later as they are smaller and ripen far more quickly. As spring warms the water, the rate of sex-cell development increases. The final

trigger for the massed event is the full moon. During the next few nights the sex cells of a large proportion of the corals on the reef are released into the sea. The number of gametes simultaneously ejected is unimaginable. Perhaps there are chemical methods whereby a sperm of one species can locate an appropriate egg in this sea of gametes. The sheer mass of cells soon exhausts the appetite of predators.

While spawning is a fascinating period for coral biologists, most divers go out of their way to avoid diving a reef that has just spawned. This is because visibility becomes so poor that diving is unenjoyable and photography impossible. There is a charming reef near Port Moresby in Papua New Guinea that I have tried to dive on several occasions, but it seems I always manage to arrive just after something or other has spawned: you cannot see a metre in front of you for all the pale globules of fertilized and unfertilized eggs floating in the water.

Once a sperm has fertilized an egg the new cnidarian is known as a planula larva. The tiny creature is, at first, attracted to light and so swims upwards, floating near the surface at the mercy of ocean currents. A few days later (or in some species as much as two months later), the planula sinks downwards. However, only a few descending planulae settle in locations where they can assume the polyp form and begin to establish a new colony.

Even if a planula settles on a suitable patch and begins to form a colony there are innumerable problems. If other corals are already established in the area they are hardly likely to greet the newcomer with open arms. The stony corals on crowded reefs are forever engaged in remorseless, slow-motion battles not only for the space available on which to grow, but also for light. Different species of coral grow at different rates, and some structures take longer to establish themselves than others. One of the fastest-growing types of coral, for example, is *Acropora*. This group includes the well-known Caribbean staghorn coral *A. cervicornis*. *Acropora* colonies will often grow quickly into flattened plate formations that will cast a slower-growing coral colony into shade. Doomed to the loss of direct sunlight, such a colony would eventually die if it did not have defence mechanisms. Slower-growing corals when thus threatened will often extrude long, tubular append-ages known as mesenterial filaments which attack and eat away at the neighbouring coral. Those areas that the filaments reach will die. If the over-growing coral is relatively small, its rival may succeed in killing it outright, and so secure its own access to the sunlight. A careful examination of the area between two neighbouring species of coral will often reveal a bleached band of dead coral belonging to one or the other, the area that has been destroyed by the other coral's mesenterial filaments. It is now known that a dominance hierarchy exists among corals in terms of their ability to attack their neighbours. Although this hierarchy prevents neighbouring corals from entering into internecine battles, a coral that is being attacked by a dominant rival on its left flank may well be simultaneously attacking a submissive rival on its right.

It was originally supposed that a simple formula was at work: slower-growing corals would tend to be dominant over their faster-growing neighbours and so manage to establish themselves. But the tale is not quite complete. At least one species of coral which is prone to damage by the mesenterial filament attack of a slower-growing neighbour is known to be able to recover and counter-attack. The Pacific *Pocillopora* can regenerate the area killed by a neighbour's mesenterial filaments. Then,

Continued on page 42

Every millimetre of reef space must be fought for. Here, on a reef in the Bahamas, a colony of hydrozoan fire coral *Millepora alcicornis* has come into contact with a purple sea fan *Gorgonia ventalina*. The sea fan is doomed. The fire coral – the beige, flame-like fingers in the centre of the fan – has destroyed part of the fan by touching, then encrusting it and smothering its tissue. This has broken away, but the beige tide of encrusting fire coral has advanced inexorably across the sea fan. Only the rich purple parts of the sea fan are still healthy; the rest is dying or already smothered. But the fire coral encrustation is itself doomed. The supple fan will be overgrown by a brittle crust of fire coral, unable to bend in the current. The more complete the fire coral's victory, the sooner it will seal its own fate and snap in the surge.

Dark-green stands of *Tubastraea micrantha* decorate a Papuan reef. These are non-reef-building (ahermatypic) corals that lack zooxanthellae. *Tubastraea* colonies can reach nearly 1.5 metres (5 feet) in height and tend to be found on deeper or poorly lit sections of reef. Here the colonies are growing in shallow water; the reef is beneath a large cliff so little direct sunlight reaches this area.

THE NATURAL HISTORY OF THE REEF

perhaps as much as two months later, this regenerated area will produce new weapons – elongated tentacles known as sweepers – which destroy any part of the neighbouring colony that they touch. Eventually *Pocillopora* will triumph and grow over its rival.

Luck determines whether a planula larva settles where it can establish a coral colony. Given the complex battles between different coral species for the available space, as well as the different shapes they can assume according to location, one can begin to understand something of the immense structural complexity of the coral reef. And yet an understanding of the stony corals is only the beginning.

NON-REEF-BUILDING CORALS

Many non-reef-building (ahermatypic) hard corals can be found on the reef. Reef-building corals cannot survive in the more shadowy corners of the reef: the overhangs, caves and caverns that lack direct sunlight. Hard corals lacking zooxanthellae thrive in such locations, however, feeding entirely on passing plankton. Examples from Pacific reefs include many of the family Dendrophylliidae. Shine a torch at the ceiling of an overhang on a night dive and you might see beautiful clusters of bright-yellow coral busily feeding with tentacles extended. These are the daisy corals *Dendrophyllia*. A close relative of these canary-yellow corals is the sombre, dark-green *Tubastraea*. This grows in bush-like shapes on the darker edges of Indo-Pacific reefs. Swim up close and you will see that the bush is in fact flattened: the coral grows at right angles to the prevailing current in order to maximize the amount of plankton it is able to catch.

Sea fans and soft corals are other ahermatypic corals found on the reef. As their names suggest, they do not secrete rigid limestone corallites. Furthermore, they lack symbiotic algae which means they must feed entirely on passing plankton. Hence soft corals are to be found in greater abundance in areas of strong currents. As with stony corals, soft corals will extend their tentacles to feed; yet many can extend far more than just their tentacles.

I remember one occasion when I was swimming along an unusually drab corner of a Red Sea reef with my dive companion. It was the first time I had dived an Indo-Pacific reef. I noticed there were few stony corals to be seen on this uninteresting stretch of relatively barren coral rock. This was somewhat surprising as only a few metres behind were bizarre canopies and buttresses of stony coral. Now everything seemed to have petered out. My dive companion then pointed out some darkly coloured blobs attached to the rock. They were small and dense and did not hold my interest for long.

I signalled to my partner and we both swam around the exposed point – where the reef jutted out into open water – to the more sheltered reef wall on the other side where stony corals were again magnificently in evidence. We pottered around for half an hour or so and began to notice that a current was slowly building up. There, among the stony corals, we were sheltered from it. Then I realized we would have to swim around that drab point again to get back to the boat. Experience told me that the current would be powering its way around the corner; but I predicted that it would be flowing in the direction of the boat and that we would be carried along without having to swim. I signalled to my partner who nodded assent and we both turned and set off towards the point. With each fin kick we moved further into the current and were carried more and more quickly. Then, as we accelerated towards the point, I felt a shudder of alarm. The current was not carrying us in the direction in which we intended to go but to another spectacular area of reef. Great billowing, metre-high, multi-coloured corals were everywhere. Some were yellow, others orange, some rich purple. Thousands of small silver fish shimmered beyond them, swimming frantically just to hold position so they could pluck plankton from the water, then bursting apart as if a bomb had been dropped among them. We saw a blur as six fish the colour of blue silver streaked through them in staggered formation. I recognized them as a species of tuna. They slowed down, hanging out the pectoral fins on one side of their bodies like the indicators on old-fashioned cars and, in perfect unison, swam off into the blue-water background. The tiny silver fish resumed their shimmering cloud formation.

We could not swim against the current; it carried us along effortlessly. I considered swimming down to the point and grabbing hold of a rock, or even one of those outrageous purple, billowing corals, and clawing my way back to the sheltered part of the reef. I turned head-on into the current in a vain attempt to swim against it, diving downwards to try to reach the receding reef. But for every metre I dived deeper, the current pushed me 3 metres further along. I was beginning to lose control of my breathing. The regulator never seemed to provide quite enough air. I lost sight of my companion.

Then the multi-hued point disappeared and I was swept along the edge of the reef. I was nearly out of air so was forced to surface in the hope that someone on the boat, wherever it was, would spot me. As I ascended I saw an anchor below on the sand and then its chain, rising at an angle of 45 degrees towards the surface. With immense relief I realized that another boat must have arrived. Hanging on to the chain a few metres below the surface and stretched horizontally by the current was my companion who, I noticed, was grinning. We broke surface together and I discovered that this was *our* dive boat. As we struggled out of our gear, my companion talked excitedly. I quickly concluded that we had indeed returned to the dive boat along the same route in which we had left it. I was initially confused, but then my partner told me that the boring blobs we saw at the start of the dive were in fact retracted soft corals: as soon as there is a current, they swell with sea water, expand and feed. No wonder I was so convinced we were travelling in a different direction in the current; the emergence of the soft corals had dramatically transformed the scene.

The soft corals that bloom in such splendid colours belong to the family Nephtheidae and are found on Indo-Pacific reefs but not on Caribbean ones. When a current is flowing across an Indo-Pacific reef these turgid soft corals transform a beautiful area into somewhere quite magical. If there is no current, the soft corals retract and shrink into tiny, inconspicuous clumps and even their colours compress into dullness. Diving a reef with a current takes a lot of effort and determination but is well worth it: a diver who chooses to dive such a reef only at times of slack water, or in areas avoided by currents, is like someone going to a concert while wearing ear-plugs and misses most of what is going on. The static backbone of the reef is provided by its stony corals; its dynamics hinge on the plankton-bearing currents. Almost everything else is directly or indirectly dependent on those currents. Thus, at the beginning of a dive a good general rule is to work your way to that part of the reef where the current is strongest.

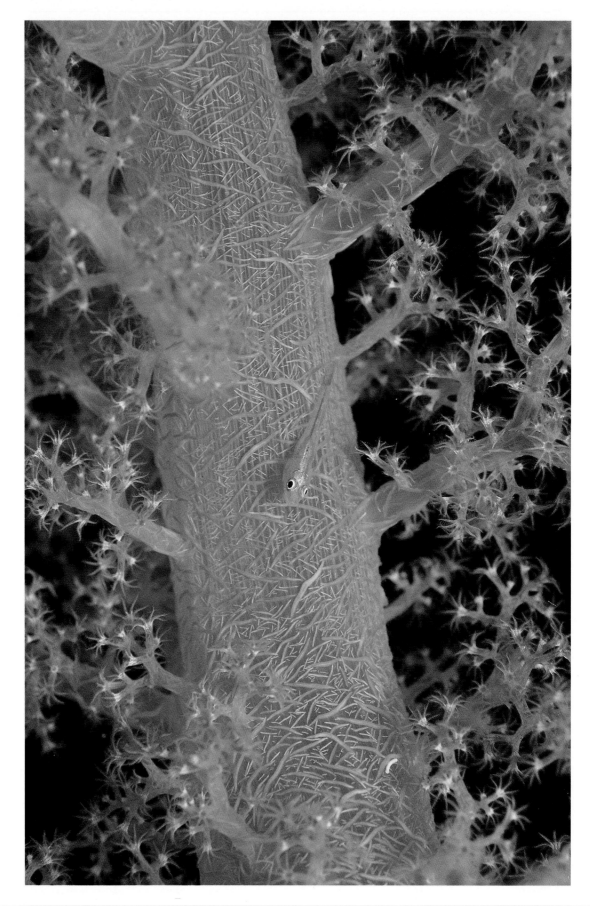

There are many other, less conspicuous, varieties of soft coral. Often drab in colour and found in areas where stony corals attract more attention, they are easily overlooked. Examples include the beige *Sinularia* and the pallid *Sarcophyton*.

Spectacular sea fans grip the reef and sway in the current like the brightly coloured sails of sunken galleons. They can vary in size from less than a metre (3 feet) in width to considerably more. I can recall an off-shore reef in the remote waters of Papua that has surrendered one entire flank to a cornucopia of sea fans. They vary from 2 metres (6½ feet) to nearer 3 metres (10 feet) across. Each is a slightly different hue to that of its neighbour: there are oranges, reds, yellows, pinks; many display colours of the spectrum so subtle that you cannot name them – some little-known blend of yellow and pink, for example, or some vague area between orange and ochre. And the colour that a sea fan appears to be at its particular depth is radically different from the colour it will assume when lit by a torch or a flash-gun.

The sea fan is a system of ever-finer branches, each covered in polyps. When these polyps are extended, a close inspection will reveal how superbly efficient they are at capturing prey. Their tentacles fill the gaps between branches and trap virtually anything the current carries their way. The polyps have an interconnected nervous system: touching just one small part of the sea fan can cause all of its polyps to retract.

The shallows of some Caribbean reefs are dominated by sea fans, particularly in areas of strong wave surge that provide a constant supply of food. The two common species in these waters are the Venus sea fan *Gorgonia flabellum*, which is a pale, lime-green colour, and the larger and more impressive purple sea fan *G. ventalina*. The sight of these lovely creatures swaying in unison to the overhead waves is majestic, but can be something of an acquired taste as I discovered while on a dive off the Florida Keys. The rough sea was causing the anchored boat to bob up and down vigorously and sway from side to side. Divers and snorkellers were preparing to submerge. The skipper of the boat suggested that if any of us were feeling seasick we should jump in as soon as possible as we would soon feel much better once in the water. One poor fellow who was feeling the worse for wear put on his mask, fins and snorkel and leapt overboard, but was back in the boat a minute later. He explained that however nauseous he felt in the rocking boat, it was infinitely better than gazing upon an expanse of sea fans swaying ceaselessly in unison to the swell.

The sea fans I have just mentioned are members of a group called the gorgonians. While most sea fans grow in flattened shapes, gorgonians are found in many other varieties. Some, the sea whips, grow as single thin stalks and are found in areas of strong currents. The direction in which they bend indicates the flow of the current, and this is the first thing divers should check when swimming down to a reef where a current is anticipated. Such important information can save a great deal of energy, air and dive time, for, once noted, the reef can be approached according to its current.

Some species of sea whip grow many stems from an initial stalk, while others blossom into complex tangles. The common names match their visual appearance: candelabrum soft coral, bushy soft coral, forked and smooth sea feathers. These sea whips dominate the underwater scenery of many Caribbean patch reefs; furthermore, they can establish themselves independently of stony corals and provide other sorts of habitat. Between the outer reef and the shore of the Florida Keys there

This close-up shot of a soft coral was taken on the reef wall of Sanganeb atoll in the Sudanese Red Sea. The feathery eight-tentacled polyps are clearly visible. The struts of calcareous scaffolding known as spicules can be seen throughout the walls of the animal. In some species of soft coral the spicules extend outwards from the polyp and serve a protective function, making the creature prohibitively bristly to the touch. This soft coral has provided a home for a tiny fish *Pleurosicya mossambica* that belongs to a large family known as the gobies. At a mere 2 centimetres (¾ of an inch) in length and perfectly coloured to match its background, this little fish is a typically inconspicuous member of the group. It uses the soft coral as a camouflage base from which to dart into open water and feed.

are many such surreal formations of sea whips in the murky water. This is a haunting world of half-seen shapes and fading shadows. One of the soft corals found here is commonly known as dead man's fingers *Briareum asbestinum*. I cannot help thinking that the person who coined the common name must have been nervously exploring such a habitat at the time.

The stony corals, soft corals, sea fans and sea whips are the major cnidarian components of the reef, and each is illustrated with photographs in Part Two. Needless to say, the situation is vastly more varied and elaborate than this introduction might suggest. Those interested in exploring the cnidarians of the reef in greater detail should refer to the Further Reading section (*see page 194*) and to the chart on pages 62-63.

PLANTS OF THE REEF

When biologists first tried to understand the ecology of coral reefs they soon ran into a problem. It hardly seemed possible that stony corals, feeding on relatively poor supplies of plankton, could not only build huge reefs, but also support an immense bulk of other creatures from higher up the food chain, such as sea urchins, worms, crabs and fish that either eat the coral or eat creatures that eat the coral. As we have seen, part of the answer lies in the role of the zooxanthellae. There is, however, another crucial factor in the equation which, although long suspected, has only recently been clarified.

Considerable areas of reef that lack the usual stony corals often seem to be painted in a pleasant, pale-purple colour. Closer inspection reveals that this colour is supplied by coral-like formations, sandwiched between living colonies of coral. They are hard to the touch, but have no polyps or other familiar features of corals. This mysterious pseudo-coral assumes a variety of shape: flat layers, overlapping crusts and small lumps. Something quite different must be in attendance.

These coral-like layers of purple are examples of another crucially important plant component of the reef known as coralline algae, a variety of red seaweed that encrusts itself with lime. Coralline algae need remarkably little sunlight in order to survive – far less than the zooxanthellae – so they are commonly found in deep and shady parts of the reef. They are also perfectly capable of establishing themselves in shallow areas that are too turbulent for stony corals, and can also exist independently of reefs. They form algal reefs, as opposed to coral reefs, in the deeper as well as the colder waters of the world.

The significance of coralline algae to the coral reef is immense. They grow quickly and act like a layer of cement which bonds coral rock together, glues loose fragments of rubble and prevents the splitting or collapse of dead coral rock. This layer provides a secure foundation for often immensely heavy formations of stony coral. Without it, the collapse rate of stony corals would be so great that many coral colonies would tumble down the reef slope and many reefs would crumble away. The coralline algae thus provide a substantial structural component of the reef. Indeed in many reefs, the bulk of the substrate consists of coralline algae, so the term 'coral' reef is not always appropriate.

The other crucial plant component of the reef is known as algal turf. Made up of tiny plants, called filamentous algae, that settle on any available space, algal turf is the staple diet of numerous reef herbivores, including snails, sea urchins and various fish. Their feeding is crucial in preventing the filamentous algae from overgrowing the corals.

There are several species of damselfish (family Pomacentridae) that actually cultivate their own gardens of filamentous algae by chasing away any rival herbivore that approaches their territory. Once the garden is established, the damselfish has a constant supply of food. Such a garden is easy to spot on a reef, looking like a close-cropped growth of green hair. Hovering fearlessly above is certain to be a drab-coloured damselfish, ever ready to defend its patch of algal turf. The aggression of such a damselfish is without equal. Forget about stories of attacks by barracuda and sharks; although its attacks are harmless to humans, the damselfish is more fearless in its onslaughts than even the great white shark *Carcharodon carcharias*.

The initial stages of a damselfish attack compare with the threat display of the grey reef shark *Carcharhinus amblyrhynchos*: exaggerated swimming and posturing motions warn of what is to follow. The damselfish will assume an unnatural position with fins splayed out and head held high. If this is ignored by the foolhardy diver then the fish will often give yet further warning of its intentions by making a thumping sound. If the diver still has not fled then attack is inevitable. The damselfish – 10 centimetres (4 inches) of unbridled fury – will launch itself upon the intruder. Perhaps it will charge head-on and bounce off the diver's wetsuit; perhaps it will pull his hair or nip him. There is only one escape: to withdraw honourably from the precious algal turf garden. Only then will the angry 'gardener' relax.

If the heroic aggression of this diminutive damselfish seems so surprising it is only because we have not yet realized just how formidable its rivals can be. If the outstanding feature of its behaviour is its bellicosity, then the outstanding feature of its lifestyle is the cultivation of its own private food supply in a world of competing browsers. The two are obviously interlinked but the success of this damselfish is a local, rather than a widespread, phenomenon of the reef. Occasionally a group of rival herbivores, such as parrotfish (family Scaridae), will swamp a damselfish's defences and feed on its garden. Neighbouring damselfish will combine to mount a counter-attack and drive the invaders away. This collective defence system requires these damselfish to grow their gardens in clusters so they can provide mutual back-up when needed. The negative side of the situation is that damselfish prevent coralline algae and new stony corals from estab-lishing themselves in such places. Coral rock used by damselfish for gardens will be structurally weak and an early victim of severe weather because it lacks the strengthening presence of coralline algae. This natural erosion keeps the extent of the gardens in check, despite the pugnaciousness of their inhabitants.

LARGER RESIDENTS

A full account of the animals to be found on the reef would be a survey of much of the animal kingdom. The invertebrates are inexhaustively in evidence. There are many species of sponges, worms, shells, moss animals, sea cucumbers, starfish, feather stars, shrimps, crabs and lobsters, as well as numerous creatures known only to specialists. Among vertebrates the most common and conspicuous are the bony fish which form the main photographic subject of Part Two. Many reefs have their resident turtles, and others their sea snakes: snakes that have flattened their tails into paddles and returned to the sea for everything but nesting. I remember one night being taken to a spot on an island off

Port Moresby in Papua New Guinea. I only had to turn on a torch to see the banded sea snakes slithering up the beach and into the undergrowth in search of nesting places. Completely unperturbed by the light, they continued determinedly on their way.

The reef has its supply of cartilaginous fish: the rays and sharks. Sand-coloured rays lie half buried in the sand, unnoticed by the diver until one erupts in panic and flaps away holding its tail high, the venomous spine pointing towards the diver in case he is some strange variety of ray-hunting shark. There is also a curious splotchy ray that swims slowly and clumsily with a round body and thick, stubby tail. The old adage repeated to divers on reefs world-wide springs to mind: never touch anything that moves so slowly that you could catch it. If the creature does not bother to escape then it does not need to do so because it has an effective defensive mechanism of some kind. This ungainly ray, commonly known as an electric ray (family Torpedinidae), has modified two sets of muscles in its disc – the flattened part of its body – into a pair of organs that can emit powerful electric shocks. It hunts by stunning fish and will defend itself by discharging its weapon against a diver. This has been measured in one species at up to 220 volts.

A diver I know was once engrossed with his video camera on a Red Sea reef. He was kneeling in the sand when he began to feel a pulsing numbness in one leg, as if he was getting pins and needles. It got worse and he thought he had a cramp coming on. He looked down to the sand and there, by his leg, was an electric ray that was in no hurry to move away from its resting place. The diver, on the other hand, wisely made a quick retreat. Perhaps the ray was discharging lower voltage warnings.

Then there are the sharks, the most enduringly fascinating predators of all. Their sinuous menace elicits a deep and ancient appreciation within the human mind that one is in the presence of predatory perfection. Any healthy Indo-Pacific reef will have its sharks. If divers are not too common a sight, the sharks will swim up to investigate them. Sharks are a kind of drug: most divers are naturally apprehensive at the thought of seeing sharks, but firsthand experience soon replaces anxiety with fascination.

In their attempts to take dramatic photographs of sharks, however, some divers have started to turn them into circus animals. They hand-feed sharks as a supposed demonstration of their bravery; but most people would claim this is a more accurate indicator of their level of intelligence. A shark cannot possibly be expected to appreciate where a piece of dead fish ends and a diver's hand or face begins, yet clenching dead fish in one's teeth is another version of the trick. The inevitable result is that divers are being bitten. A variation on this theme is to put on a protective chain-mail suit and then, by offering bait, to try to get a shark to bite the suit. This then results in dramatic 'shark attack' photographs. Whatever one thinks of this kind of sensationalism, it ought to be remembered that these divers are in effect training the sharks of certain reefs to bite humans. The next divers to turn up on those reefs will not be in protective suits.

Sharks come in an impressive variety of shapes and sizes, and each species has adopted a method of feeding suitable for its needs. The sluggish, heavy-bodied nurse sharks (family Ginglymostomatidae) are commonly seen at rest during the day under coral canopies. During the night they will leave their hiding places and search the reef floor for sleeping fish, lobsters, crabs and octopuses. Grey reef sharks *Carcharhinus amblyrhynchos* tend to feed at dawn and dusk. These unpredictable

A southern stingray *Dasyatis americana* rests on the sand at the edge of a Bahamian reef. Stingrays are the most commonly seen cartilaginous fish on western Atlantic reefs. They will normally remain still, trusting in their camouflage. If alarmed, however, a southern stingray may swim away curving from left to right, its tail held high and its defensive, venomous spine pointing towards the threat. Many large sharks feed on rays, and have spines embedded in their jaw and under-side to prove it.

Sharks are the predators at the apex of the reef food chain. Some reefs play host to occasional giant groupers, such as the mighty brindlebass *Epinephelus lanceolatus* of the Indo-Pacific that can attain a length of three metres (10 feet) and a weight of over 400 kilogrammes (880 pounds). These goliaths are rare, however, while sharks of numerous species are common on healthy reefs and can grow considerably larger. This whitetip reef shark *Triaenodon obesus*, calmly swimming along the wall of Osprey reef in the Coral Sea, was characteristically indifferent to my presence. Perhaps the most exasperating encounter with a shark for me was on an occasion when I was diving in Solomon Islands. I was the first into the water on a reef that had not been previously dived. As I rolled in, I noticed a large shape next to me. I assumed another diver had entered the water at the same time as me and did not bother to check. I inspected my camera and prepared to descend. Then I glanced sideways and saw a 2.5-metre (8-foot) silky shark *Carcharhinus falciformis* staring at me in amazement. The silky is a sleek and beautiful open-water species of shark. By the time I had set up my camera, the shark had moved away.

hunters should be treated with considerable respect, and neither followed nor in any way harassed. They will scavenge if they find suitable carrion, and hunt singly or in packs, targeting schools of fish for an easier kill.

In tropical waters there are two contenders for the crown of giant shark predator. The first is the tiger shark *Galeocerdo cuvier*, a widespread and common predator that thinks nothing of eating grey reef sharks in its enormously varied diet. It grows to at least 5.5 metres (18 feet) and possibly far more. With its huge mouth and stubby, serrated teeth, the tiger shark will feed on just about anything; fortunately for divers it tends to stay in deeper waters during the day. A friend of mine has the unenviable skill of bumping into tiger sharks on reefs; the result is always the same: she bites through her mouthpiece in terror!

The other massive shark predator of tropical waters is the great hammerhead *Sphyrna mokarran*, which is also likely to reach over 5.5 metres (18 feet) in length. Its favourite meal seems to be stingrays. A Sudanese fisherman once told me of how, when he was a young man, he used to wade in the thigh-deep water off Suakin, the ancient and now ruined port south of Port Sudan in the Red Sea. He and his friends would be using finely meshed nets to catch shrimps. Occasionally an enormous dorsal fin would appear, slicing through the surface towards them. Its shape and height, similar to that of a male killer whale *Orcinus orca*, would inform them that it belonged to a great hammerhead. Behind the tail they would see a murky corridor of stirred-up sand as the shark forced its bulk across the shallow, sandy bottom. The action of pulling the nets through the water, and the dancing of the shrimps trapped within would have sent vibrations across the lagoon that bore some resemblance to those caused by a large ray. The fishermen would drop their nets and stand, absolutely motionless, watching the approach of the great, grey, swaying dorsal fin of the hammerhead with stifled terror. Eventually, with no more vibrations to guide it, the shark would give up and cruise off.

THE CONSERVATION ISSUES

Over the last few years there has been a considerable increase in public awareness of the importance of conservation. The general health of the world's reefs and the outlook for their future are subjects which have been brought into sharp focus by this growing environmental concern. One can argue for the preservation of the reef for its own sake, but evidence has recently come to light which has prompted an anthropocentric reasoning behind calls for reef conservation.

The Earth's atmosphere acts like a giant greenhouse. Short-wave energy from the sun passes through the atmosphere and strikes our planet. Much of this energy is reflected back off the surface of the planet as long-wave radiation. The atmosphere contains certain 'greenhouse' gases — notably carbon dioxide, methane, water vapour and nitrous oxide — that absorb and trap this long-wave radiation. This results in the warming of the atmosphere; without greenhouse gases it is estimated that the temperature of the Earth's surface would be some 30°C (54°F) colder than it is.

There is considerable fear and mounting evidence that the Earth is getting unnaturally hot: unseasonable weather patterns, severe and persistent droughts and rising sea levels are all evidence that things are changing for the worse. Although some people with a vested interest in

Continued on page 54

AN INFINITE VARIETY OF FORM

Here, on a reef in Papua New Guinea, the cracks, gullies and clumps of dead coral rock have been overgrown with many different corals, sponges and other animals. This is an area of strong currents, indicated by the resilient short and squat shapes of the majority of these corals. In the central gully (1) such a form has been adopted by this species of *Pocillopora* (probably *P. eydouxi*) to withstand the current and swell. *Pocillopora* corals grow in more fragile and expanded formations on deeper, less turbulent parts of the reef. The *Acropora* corals are the polymorphic champions of the reef. Here (2) a typical example of a compact variety has taken up station. To the left (3) are several small clumps of *Porites* coral (possibly *P. lutea*). *Porites* corals often form dense, massive formations; this boulder-shaped coral rock may once have been such a colony, now partially destroyed by a variety of invading creatures. The highest colony in the picture (4) – probably another variety of *Acropora* – has confounded its neighbours and grown in a more fragile tree-shaped or arborescent structure. At its base (5) is a small, dense coral colony,

possibly belonging to the *Platygyra* genus. In the right-hand foreground (6) is a dense stand of *Acropora palifera*, which can withstand considerable wave action and is often dominant in areas of strong swell and current. Immediately behind it (7) is an encrusting coral colony – one that grows over the substrate – which in this case is composed of dead coral rock. The species of encrusting coral is possibly *Porites lichen*. It has assumed a haphazard growth form of irregular, stocky columns sprouting from a flat base. The dead remains of a small *Acropora* plate coral (8) have been cemented in place by purple-coloured coralline algae. Several colonies of the soft coral *Sarcophyton trocheliophorum* (9) are visible above. Ascidians – filter-feeding animals – can also be seen (10). These small, pale-green, bulb-shaped creatures belong to the species *Didemnum molle*, typically found in colonies. Despite their simple appearance, ascidians have at least one advanced characteristic: the rudimentary beginnings of a backbone present in the tadpole larvae. A variety of sponges (11) can also be seen in the picture.

preserving the status quo insist that proof is not yet at hand, it now seems undeniable that the planet is no longer in a state of balance and that we are the cause of the problem. By vastly increasing the concentrations of greenhouse gases we are allowing the atmosphere to trap yet more and more heat. The worst culprit is probably carbon dioxide which is released in colossal amounts by the burning of fossil fuels and trees. There are, however, many other greenhouse gases: the chloroflourocarbons (CFCs) that are remorselessly 'eating away' at the protective ozone layer also make highly efficient and long-lasting greenhouse gases. Forty greenhouse gases have been identified to date; and new gases are produced each year, by-products of the latest industrial processes, whose ability to trap long-wave radiation is unknown.

Coral reefs are thought to have two beneficial roles to play in terms of the greenhouse effect. Firstly, carbon dioxide, the major greenhouse gas, dissolves into sea water and becomes carbonic acid. However, the method by which coral reef animals and many other shell-building marine creatures (especially among the plankton) build up their limestone cases actually absorbs huge amounts of carbonic acid. If these creatures flourish then they will buffer the acidity of the oceans and indirectly reduce the amount of atmospheric carbon dioxide.

What would happen if this system broke down? Suppose the amount of atmospheric carbon dioxide were to increase unchecked. There may well come a time when the shell-depositing marine creatures can no longer buffer the ocean's acidity. If acidity were to rise, the shells of the plankton would begin to weaken and dissolve. This would liberate the trapped carbonate – the form in which the carbon compound is incorporated in the shell – back into the sea. As the equilibrium between carbonic acid and shell deposition broke down, the system would accelerate towards ever greater levels of marine acidity. The shells and cases of other, larger creatures, such as crustaceans and corals, would soon begin to dissolve, further increasing levels of acidity in the sea.

The second environmental benefit to be gained from coral reefs is the considerable protection they provide for the land against the sea. A coral reef can reduce mighty ocean surges to a flat calm in its lagoon. If, as some scientists predict, the exacerbation of the greenhouse effect causes sea levels to rise through the melting of polar ice and the warming and subsequent expansion of the volume of ocean water, then many low-lying areas will be submerged. Where there are healthy coral reefs, however, the shore will be protected against the full force of the ocean, provided that the upward growth of the reefs can keep pace with the rise in sea level. In areas where people have destroyed local reefs by, for example, mining the reefs' limestone for building material, the effect on the suddenly unprotected coastline has been devastating.

If the coral reefs perish, the significance of their disappearance will be far greater than the death of the richest marine ecosystems. There has been a long-standing debate about the way in which oceans manage to keep their salt concentrations constant despite the unending supply of minerals carried into the sea by rivers. Coral reefs may be the explanation. Many of the reef flats and lagoons of today's reefs will become tomorrow's evaporation basins, areas where water evaporates leaving behind an expanse of salt crystals. It appears that this regulatory process, which removes salt from the sea as more pours in, is by no means new. If this is indeed the way in which the seas manage to control their salt content, then reefs must continue to prosper. A rise in sea levels could disrupt the system as many of these salt basins would then be flooded, thus liberating vast concentrations of salt back into the sea that could only be inimical to the biological health of the oceans. We cannot begin to calculate the effect on the oceans if they were to lose their most diverse communities. Besides the threat posed by the exacerbation of the greenhouse effect, however, reefs face constant abuse from the modern world. I will briefly outline the worst offenders.

The clearing of tropical rain forest is an environmental issue currently the focus of much publicity. But how many people realize that this process is often directly damaging to coral reefs? Without trees to anchor the soil it is washed away by rain. Rivers carry huge amounts of sediment into the sea and local reefs are suffocated. Pollution damage is also a problem where industrial waste and untreated human waste are pumped straight into the sea. The run-off from land fertilizers is equally disastrous, flowing over reefs and encouraging the growth of algae which eventually choke the coral backbone. In this way it can take only a few weeks for a healthy coral reef to become a dull bank of marine algae; and once the algae are in place and the corals dead, the algae are there to stay. The fishing industry also causes problems: it is common practice for fishermen around the world to use explosives to catch fish. It takes little imagination to realize the devastating effect dynamite has on coral reefs. The transportation of goods by sea is often a hazard to reefs as ships and boats are forever running into and damaging them world-wide. Imagine the result of a fully-laden supertanker breaking its back on a reef in the narrow Red Sea. One need only remember the effect of the *Exxon Valdez* coming to grief in Alaska's Prince William Sound in 1989, and then transport that scenario of ecological devastation to a remote part of the reef-rich Red Sea where there are no immediate methods of recovering (or pretending to recover) the vast oil slick that would result, and no immediate likelihood of its break up. The latter would be especially true if the wrecking happened during the hot and windless summer months when the sea is flat and calm. The slick would merely drift, coating and killing everything it encountered. There is already considerable pollution in the Red Sea. I remember surveying a beach a few kilometres downwind from a couple of Egyptian oil platforms. The crude oil and assorted industrial junk had coated the beach in a layer 50 centimetres (20 inches) deep. Given the modest size of the island, it was depressing to imagine how much more petroleum-based filth was surreptitiously passing into the sea from those two rigs alone. Some oil tankers will inevitably continue to flush out their tanks at sea; and we can only impotently hope that a laden supertanker does not come to grief.

The leisure and tourism industries are also responsible for inflicting damage to coral reefs. Alterations to the coastline caused by the construction of harbours and marinas, and by dredging, for example, can cause drastic variations in the currents that feed a nearby reef and it will suffer accordingly. Then there is an international trade in removing items such as corals, shells, turtles and various fish from reefs, and either selling their dried remains in local tourist shops, or exporting them for sale in foreign countries. It has been estimated that some 1,500 tonnes of coral are imported annually into the USA in this way; and much of it has been illegally removed from the reefs of the Philippines. Absurdly, while tourist shops in Florida are not allowed to sell coral souvenirs plundered from Florida's reefs, they happily sell corals illegally removed and imported from Pacific reefs instead.

Continued on page 58

Overleaf
Large areas of western Atlantic reefs are now showing signs of stress. One of the first corals to bleach and die in these waters is the beautiful, but fragile elkhorn coral *Acropora palmata*. Here, on this Bahamian reef, huge areas of elkhorn have died, their skeletons quickly being settled upon by algae. The beige elkhorn colony in the centre is still alive, though closer inspection reveals bleached patches. We found the remains of a large wreck on this reef which may have caused the death of the corals. Pollutants from the wreck may have escaped onto them; or other factors, such as unusually high water temperatures, may have been responsible.

Diving is another increasingly popular leisure activity which can threaten the health of coral reefs. An anchor, anchor chain, clumsy kick of a fin, or hand reaching out to grab hold of something, all spell doom for coral. When many people are diving the same reefs, the deterioration of those reefs is dramatic. The most heavily abused reefs in the world may well be those off southern Florida. These are not only suffering from pollution from the mainland, but they are also enduring the remorseless visits of divers and fishermen. Disruption in the balance of creatures on a reef by over-fishing can also cause a massive detrimental impact to the entire system. If the herbivores are removed, for instance, algal growth will proceed unchecked. An attempt to ban fishing on these threatened reefs would probably provoke a civil war as fishing is the most popular sport in Florida. On a sunny weekend you can hardly see the reefs of John Pennekamp State Park for the boats above. It has been estimated that as many as a million people annually explore these waters. Even if moorings are used to avoid anchor damage and a code of practice for divers is enforced, accidents will continue to happen. The sad fact is that no one is more concerned with the preservation of their reefs than the people of Florida. It has been said that if these reefs manage to survive the pollution of the mainland, they will ultimately be loved to death by their visitors.

There are also pressures on the reef that would appear at first glance to be natural. An example is the now regular infestations of Australian reefs by the coral-eating crown-of-thorns starfish *Acanthaster planci*, though it has been suggested that such population explosions could be the result of human interference in the ecological balance. When their numbers are great enough – as they often are – these starfish will eat an entire living reef. Furthermore, in 1983, as much as 99 per cent of the Caribbean sea urchin *Diadema antillarum* population was reported to have died in many areas. These are vital browsers of the reef's algal turf and, in their absence, algal growth exploded on Caribbean reefs.

What does the future hold for the world's coral reefs? It is a daunting question. We saw earlier that corals deposit their limestone most efficiently within a very limited temperature range. We have also seen that most scientists now predict that global warming will take place due to the exacerbation of the greenhouse effect, leading to warmer seas. In these conditions, reefs may not be able to continue laying down their skeletons at a rate greater than that at which they are eroded.

There is another ominous threat to reefs connected with rising sea temperatures that has recently come to light. Coral colonies have been known to occasionally lose their zooxanthellae. The ability of the zooxanthellae to produce oxygen by photosynthesis increases with temperature. It appears that if the zooxanthellae produce too much oxygen during photosynthesis, then toxic by-products result that are damaging to the tissues of the coral polyp. Thus, the zooxanthellae may be lost through the damaged wall of the polyp back into the ocean. The coral colony turns brilliant white as it now lacks any pigmentation. The process is known as coral bleaching. Close inspection of a bleached coral colony at night will reveal that coral polyps are still present, but transparent. Such a coral may recover by obtaining new zooxanthellae from the surrounding water but it is more likely, however, that it will die.

Outbreaks of coral bleaching have been recorded world-wide and cover enormous tracts of reef. At least three major occurrences since 1979 have been reported by researchers. Particularly alarming is the fact that episodes of bleaching coincide with either the hottest season for that area, or unusually hot local conditions due to other factors. The threat is clear: global warming means warmer seas; and warmer seas may cause coral bleaching and the widespread death of reefs.

Coral reefs, then, are in peril both on the grand and local scale. As divers are capable of inflicting damage on reefs, it could be argued that a book such as this, that might encourage others to take up reef diving, is hardly a positive contribution. Certainly for me a healthy coral reef is the *non plus ultra* of diving; but to dive reefs oneself and hope to dissuade others from doing the same is an absurd hypocrisy.

To begin with, we must examine the ways in which divers harm reefs. Blunt as it sounds, the worst offenders are novice divers who tend to thrash about having yet to learn to control their buoyancy and co-ordination. This is hardly their fault, but rather the result of competitive diving organizations making it forever easier for people to gain diving certification. The cut-throat competition liberates more and more clumsy divers onto the most fragile of marine ecosystems. These thoughts will doubtless outrage some people; but how many experienced reef divers can honestly deny that as beginners they were allowed on reefs too soon, or claim not to have seen hapless novices blundering and crunching their way through coral? When they return to the boat, these novices feel mortified with themselves without realizing that they are not directly to blame.

The industrialized world is like a giant, insatiable, parasitic octopus straddling the planet. Worse still, it is incontinent, forever discharging greater amounts of its indelible black ink. Meanwhile its tentacles set off on yet more ambitious pilgrimages, ever eager to link up in more and more remote areas and knot themselves together. Only the most ruthless of scientists would claim that it is part of the task of 'progress' to show that any other outlook on the world is archaic. And yet this octopus, science's deformed offspring, is unquestionably its most enduring achievement. Our standards of living have certainly improved enormously over the last 100 years but the consequences are possibly catastrophic. The increased interest in wilderness exploration is a desperate attempt to re-establish our links with a world haunted with beauty, fear and fascination. The coral reef is the perfect symbol. Peerlessly beautiful, desperately fragile, immensely intricate and with a significance far beyond its own borders, it is furthermore one of the finest examples of a recycling and therefore virtually self-sustaining ecosystem in Nature.

There are many things being done – sadly all too often on only the local scale – to protect reefs. However, wider, and more costly measures must now be put into operation in order to halt the damage. Marine parks must become much more widespread. The unending destruction by fishermen must be curtailed. Considerable tracts of reef must be forbidden to any humans. Funds must be made available for research and conservation methods to be brought to and sustained at a feverish pitch.

More and more divers are beginning to see that to dive a coral reef is to realize the bond that exists between the survival of the reef and the responsibility of its visitors to protect it. Diving can no longer be considered as just another seaside activity on a par with windsurfing, sunbathing and water-skiing. It is rather the opportunity to gain a first-hand insight into the fact that what exists beneath the waves must continue to do so.

Overleaf
Two of the smaller fish residents of a well-developed Bahamian reef stare out of their shelter. The fish with the pale blue spots is a small grouper known as a coney *Cephalopholis fulvus*. It comes in various distinctive colour patterns including a bright-yellow version. The fish with the yellow head is an angelfish known as a rockbeauty *Holacanthus tricolor*; this is the only colour scheme of the adult. The rockbeauty is territorial and will guard its corner of the reef against rivals. The coney, however, does not pose any threat to the angelfish and so the two can exist side by side.

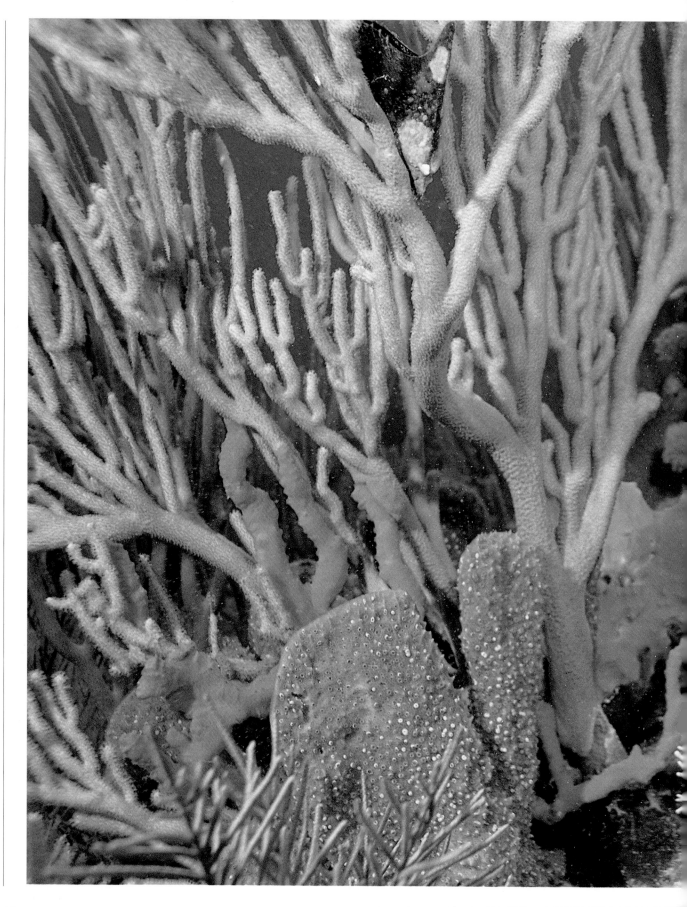

REEF CNIDARIANS

Corals, jellyfish and anemones of the reef community belong to the phylum Cnidaria. This chart looks at the zoological classification of animals within this phylum that can be found on the reef.

PHYLUM CNIDARIA

CLASS

HYDROZOA

Includes freshwater polyps and certain forms of jellyfish, including the dreaded Portugese Man-of-War *Physalia*. Hydroids are commonly found in areas of strong currents on the reef and can deliver a powerful sting to an unwary diver. The fire corals *Millepora*, commonly found on reefs, belong to this group. Their ability to sting is well known to careless divers.

Portugese Man-of-War *Physalia*

ANTHOZOA

By far the most important cnidarians on the reef. The class is divided as follows:

SUB-CLASS

SCYPHOZOA

Jellyfish that have a typical, bell-shaped appearance with tentacles extruding from within the bell, belong to this group. They are not often found on the reef unless carried there by currents. The upside-down jellyfish *Cassiopea* can occur in considerable numbers on sheltered, shallow stretches of lagoon. Here it basks with its tentacles, which contain photosynthesizing algae, held towards the surface.

Upside-down jellyfish *Cassiopea*

CUBOZOA

These are the box jellyfish. They are cube-shaped with four sets of tentacles extending from the lower corners of the cube. The sea-wasp *Chironex* of the north-east coast of Australia has a sting which can be fatal to humans. During the summer months it is advisable to stay out of the murky inshore waters.

Sea-wasp *Chironex*

ZOANTHARIA

These are the hexacorals, the polyps of which have six, or multiples of six, tentacles. The following orders are relevant to the reef:

Zoantharian polyps

ALCYONARIA

These are the octocorals, the polyps of which have eight tentacles. The following orders are relevant to the reef:

Octocoral polyp

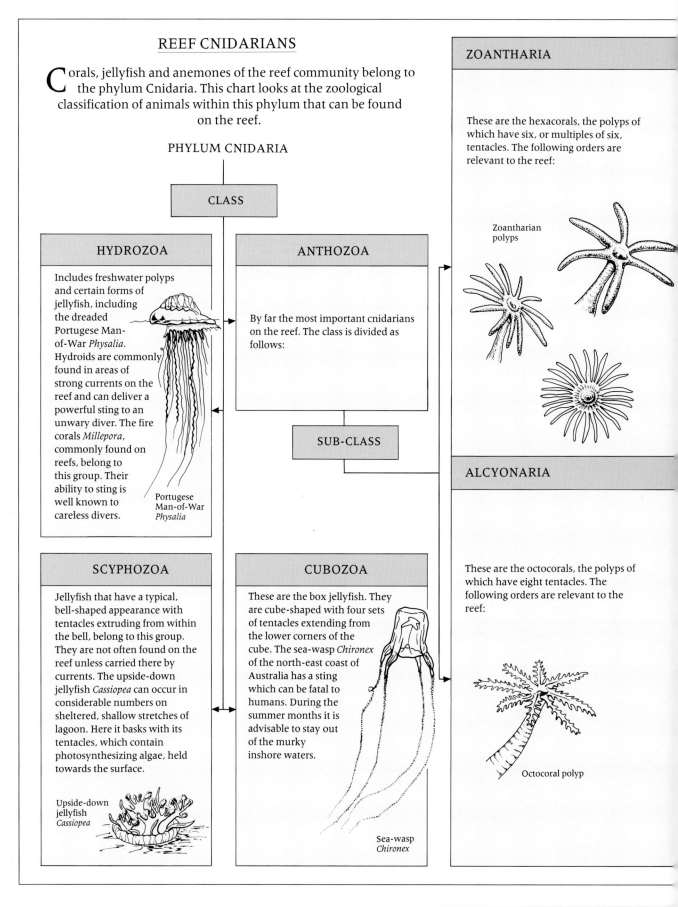

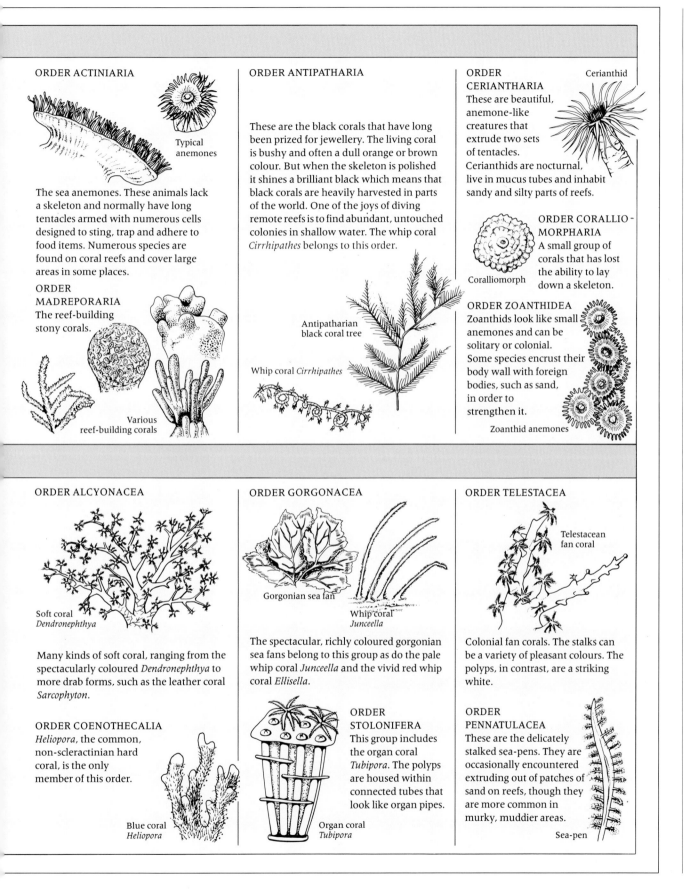

ORDER ACTINIARIA

Typical anemones

The sea anemones. These animals lack a skeleton and normally have long tentacles armed with numerous cells designed to sting, trap and adhere to food items. Numerous species are found on coral reefs and cover large areas in some places.

ORDER MADREPORARIA
The reef-building stony corals.

Various reef-building corals

ORDER ANTIPATHARIA

These are the black corals that have long been prized for jewellery. The living coral is bushy and often a dull orange or brown colour. But when the skeleton is polished it shines a brilliant black which means that black corals are heavily harvested in parts of the world. One of the joys of diving remote reefs is to find abundant, untouched colonies in shallow water. The whip coral *Cirrhipathes* belongs to this order.

Antipatharian black coral tree

Whip coral *Cirrhipathes*

ORDER CERIANTHARIA
Cerianthid

These are beautiful, anemone-like creatures that extrude two sets of tentacles. Cerianthids are nocturnal, live in mucus tubes and inhabit sandy and silty parts of reefs.

ORDER CORALLIO-MORPHARIA
A small group of corals that has lost the ability to lay down a skeleton.

Coralliomorph

ORDER ZOANTHIDEA
Zoanthids look like small anemones and can be solitary or colonial. Some species encrust their body wall with foreign bodies, such as sand, in order to strengthen it.

Zoanthid anemones

ORDER ALCYONACEA

Soft coral *Dendronephthya*

Many kinds of soft coral, ranging from the spectacularly coloured *Dendronephthya* to more drab forms, such as the leather coral *Sarcophyton*.

ORDER COENOTHECALIA
Heliopora, the common, non-scleractinian hard coral, is the only member of this order.

Blue coral *Heliopora*

ORDER GORGONACEA

Gorgonian sea fan

Whip coral *Junceella*

The spectacular, richly coloured gorgonian sea fans belong to this group as do the pale whip coral *Junceella* and the vivid red whip coral *Ellisella*.

ORDER STOLONIFERA
This group includes the organ coral *Tubipora*. The polyps are housed within connected tubes that look like organ pipes.

Organ coral *Tubipora*

ORDER TELESTACEA

Telestacean fan coral

Colonial fan corals. The stalks can be a variety of pleasant colours. The polyps, in contrast, are a striking white.

ORDER PENNATULACEA
These are the delicately stalked sea-pens. They are occasionally encountered extruding out of patches of sand on reefs, though they are more common in murky, muddier areas.

Sea-pen

PART TWO

A JOURNEY THROUGH THE CORAL WORLD

A photographic survey of an ecological system as complex as a coral reef must be highly selective. What follows is, inevitably, a subjective collection because the fish included are, for me at least, exemplars of particular themes. One might think that underwater photographers record more or less the same things. This is rarely so. Some develop fascinations for one scale of photography, such as close-up shots, others for a more wide-angle approach. I remember once diving with someone who was only interested in photographing the brightly coloured sea slugs known as nudibranchs. The rest of us were going to feed the reef sharks, but he was not interested. Indeed, during our shark feed I spotted him half stuck in a crevice as he hunted for his beloved sea slugs; he never even glanced towards the sharks. I, on the other hand, am quite incapable of spotting a sea slug so busy am I in my quest to photograph reef fish.

There is a general progression in Part Two both in terms of the animals and habitats covered. With the animals we begin with the invertebrates and then progress to the bony fish and the cartilaginous fish; in terms of habitat, we journey from the lagoon to the various parts of the reef, finishing with a momentary glance into the abyssal depths beneath. The introduction of various themes such as coloration, mating, feeding and defence, should be self-explanatory.

◁ Sponges (phylum Porifera) come in many shapes and sizes. There are some 5,000 recorded species distributed throughout the world's oceans, from the coldest Arctic and Antarctic waters to the warmest shallows of the tropics. Many species have adapted to life on the reef and few are more impressive than the bright orange elephant ear sponge *Phakellia aruensis*. This one – 1.5 metres (5 feet) in height – was photographed on a reef in Papua New Guinea.

On a shallow reef off Long Island in the Bahamas, a pair of ocean surgeonfish *Acanthurus bahianus* cruises through a setting dominated by a variety of common Caribbean soft corals. Surgeonfish derive their name from the scalpel-sharp defensive spines they carry, one on each side of their body. These are retracted into sheaths when not in use, visible in front of the white, vertical bar before the tail of each fish. Surgeonfish are important grazers of the reef's algal turf. There are only small colonies of stony coral visible here; immediately behind the leading fish is some star coral *Montastrea cavernosa*. Most of the animals are soft corals: behind the second fish are some pale purple dead man's fingers *Briareum asbestinum*. The green soft corals in the central top portion of the photograph are a variety of sea rods *Plexaurella*.

◁ Corals of the genus *Acropora* are unrivalled not only in terms of their abundance but also in the variety and magnificence of their architectural forms. Here, apart from the white-fringed plate corals *Montipora* extending back from the lower right-hand corner of this photograph, virtually every coral belongs to the *Acropora* group. Given their ability to grow rapidly and assume a wide range of shapes, *Acropora* corals dominate many shallow reefs. I was not, however, diving this particular reef in Milne Bay, Papua New Guinea, in order to photograph its splendid hard corals. During a dive exactly four years previously I had encountered a 10-metre (33-foot) whale shark *Rhincodon typus* on this same point. While taking this shot I had the distinct impression that something was watching me . . .

Overleaf
Turning quickly around and looking into the blue water beyond the reef, I immediately saw, to my amazement, yet another whale shark powering towards me. For a moment I wondered if it was my old friend, but then realized that this beast, at a mere 5 metres (16 feet) in length, was something of a youngster. It was accompanied by a cluster of suckerfish *Echeneis naucrates* that immediately swam up to me to investigate. The whale shark swept past and vanished along the reef. These harmless, mighty creatures are the largest fish in the sea and will often approach a diver for a quick inspection. Whale sharks have, however, been observed feeding on small tuna, and there is the old story of a pair of boots being found in the stomach of a whale shark.

▽ Sea fans provide a habitat for many other creatures. The coloration of this 8-centimetre (3-inch) long-nosed hawkfish *Oxycirrhites typus* blends perfectly with its sea fan home. Here it waits in ambush, ready to dash out and snatch small fish and crustaceans from the current. The long-nosed hawkfish is fairly common on the deeper sea fans of Indo-Pacific reefs; finding them is a question of knowing where (and how closely) to look.

Just beneath the cliff of an island off the coast of Papua New Guinea are underwater mounds of rock. The submarine rock-face is in constant shade so stony corals cannot establish themselves. The current, however, is channelled through the alleys and fissures between rock and cliff, providing a concentrated supply of plankton and an ideal setting for sea fans. These have grown without overlapping for a simple reason: if a sea fan up-current has already filtered out the plankton, then a sea fan behind it will not gain enough nourishment to grow in that path. ▷

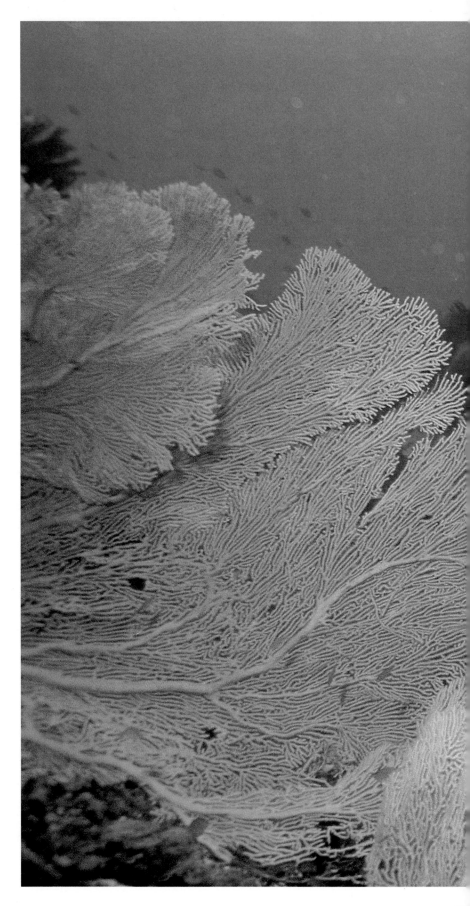

Sea fans of the family Melithaeidae can grow to impressive size if the current brings them a rich enough food supply. This one was photographed on a reef in Papua New Guinea at a depth of 30 metres (100 feet). I wanted something large to set beside this sea fan to give an impression of its size, so I buried a dead fish at its base. Within a minute this majestic 2.5-metre (8-foot) silvertip shark *Carcharhinus albimarginatus* came swooping in from down-current. Beneath the tail of the shark, a cluster of black feather stars (crinoids) has climbed up the sea fan to feed in the current.

The soft corals *Dendronephthya* spp. seem to add an other-worldly loveliness to Indo-Pacific reefs. Because they lack zooxanthellae, they are often found in ill-lit or dark parts of the reef, blossoming from underneath dead plates of coral or festooning narrow alleys of dead coral with their colours. There is a channel into the lagoon of an atoll reef in the Egyptian Red Sea that is a Mecca for soft corals. The area is lifeless when the tide is slack, and gloomy as the lagoon empties its sandy burden of murky water back into the sea. But when the tide flows in, bringing plankton-rich water from the sea beyond, the soft corals respond: gaps and cracks of coral rock are filled with their colours.

The channels into the otherwise sealed lagoons of oceanic atolls can be areas of immense currents. On one occasion while diving Osprey atoll off the Australian coast, inclement weather forced our dive boat to shelter in the lagoon. Several divers, including myself, decided to explore the current-gouged floor of the channel. We were carried along by the current on our dive out into the channel and had quite a struggle on the way back. Once we reached the deepest, fiercest stretch of current we were rewarded by the impressive sight of huge, solitary soft tree corals *Dendronephthya* sp. locked into the channel floor. This 1.75-metre (5-foot) whitetip reef shark *Triaenodon obesus* made considerably easier headway through the powerful current than the clumsy, struggling divers.

Overleaf
There is a variety of cnidarians commonly known as sea whips. The prettiest belong to the genus *Ellisella* and have bright-red stems that take on a pink appearance when the white polyps are extended. Here, on a reef in Kimbe Bay, Papua New Guinea, an impressive collection of sea whips rests during the tranquil gap between currents.

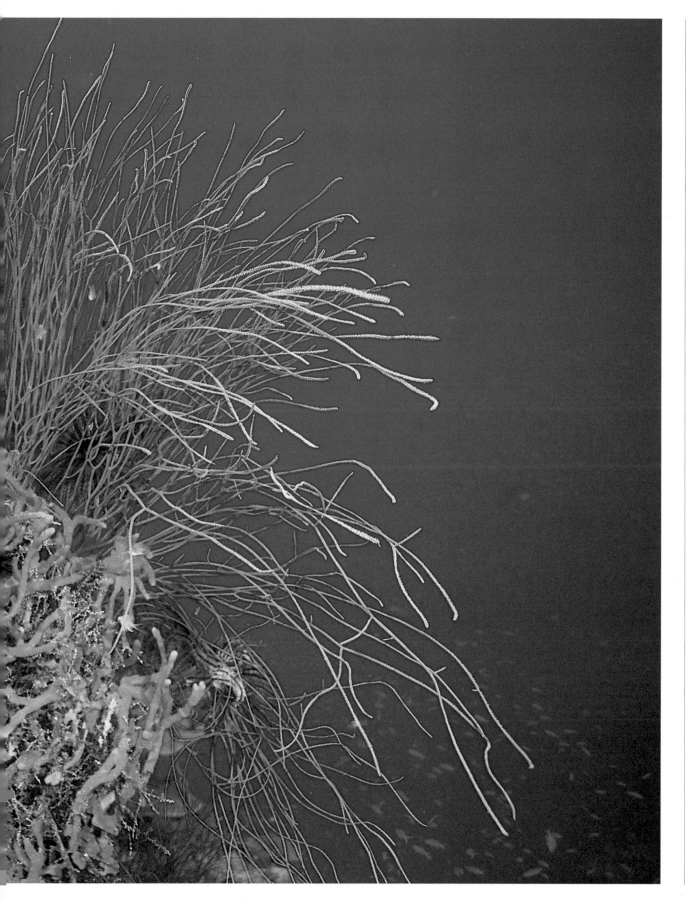

◁ A close look between the sea whip stems reveals a surprise. A razor-fish *Centriscus* sp. hovers in typical head-down posture. This fish is about 8 centimetres (3 inches) in length, and belongs to an extraordinary group. The body is protected by a rigid casing that, with its sharp edges, gives rise to the common name. Razor-fish rarely deviate from their strange head-down posture and even swim sideways in this unlikely position. They are usually encountered in schools of several dozen, bobbing up and down in unison. It is certainly a stance that makes them look completely unlike fish and is likely to make both predators and prey ignore them. Their elongated, delicate mouths look as if they are designed to pluck tiny crustaceans out of the most inaccessible of hiding places.

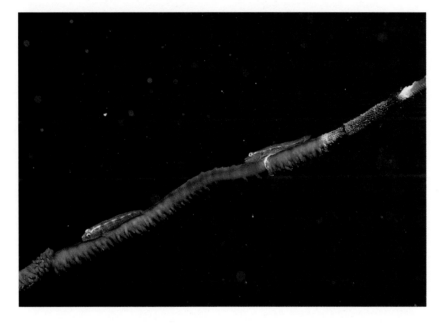

△ This antipatharian whip coral *Cirrhipathes* in the Red Sea, has a mated pair of tiny gobies *Bryaninops yongei* in residence. They are about 2 centimetres (¾ of an inch) in length. The pelvic fins – the paired fins on the underbelly – work as a suction device with which the fish can attach themselves to whip corals, their permanent home, even in strong currents. The whip coral extends away from the reef and into the food-rich open water. The gobies will dart out and snatch miniscule crustaceans that pass by, and then return to the whip coral before any predator notices their movements. Behind the upper goby is an area cleared of whip coral tissue; here the grey eggs of the fish can be seen in a cluster. Perhaps the gobies strip the tissue from the coral, or use areas already cleared by other creatures such as feather stars for depositing their eggs.

◁ The current flows past an overhanging coral formation on a Papuan reef and a niche of intense filter-feeding activity results. Several silver, black and red feather stars have clambered onto sea fans to filter-feed from optimum vantage points. The white and purple bag-like animal to the immediate left of a small green sponge (*upper centre*), is a filter-feeding ascidian *Polycarpa aurata*. Ascidians inhabit the taxonomic middle ground between invertebrates and vertebrates as they have the beginnings of a backbone in the free-swimming, larval stage of development. Immediately above and to the left of the ascidian are clusters of solitary yellow daisy corals *Tubastraea*. A large, grey, cauliflower-like soft coral *Nephthya* sp. is visible at the top of the picture; an angelfish *Euxiphipops navarchus* hovers at the bottom.

△ A mantis shrimp *Odontodactylus scyllarus* moves at dusk across the rubble-strewn sea bed inshore of a Papuan reef. At only 12 centimetres (5 inches) in length it might seem a harmless enough creature. But the speed of the mantis shrimp's offensive strike is far faster than the eye can see. Tucked under the front of its body, like the upside-down hammers on a double-barrelled flintlock pistol, are a pair of appendages known as the second maxillipeds. The speed with which these strike forwards to smash any rival or prey in front of the shrimp is the fastest-known movement in the animal kingdom. The strike has been timed at under four milliseconds. This miniature bully of the underwater landscape belongs to an order of crustaceans named the Stomatopoda of which there are many species. They are divided into the smashers, that use their weapons to smash through the armour of crabs, shrimps and snails; and the piercers, that use more sharply pointed maxillipeds to impale fish. Because of the ease with which mantis shrimps can damage a rival, they have evolved a complex matrix of warning behaviour designed to keep their internecine battles to a minimum. This fearless individual demonstrated a profound knowledge of the terrain on which I found it. It was originally peeping out from under a rock. When I moved the rock, it slowly and confidently set off across the bottom. I kept pace. After moving in a straight line for about 20 metres (65 feet) it suddenly sped off at high speed at a right angle to its original direction for another 10 metres (33 feet) and plunged straight down a burrow. Only then did I realize that it had been leading me along its escape route.

◁ I was diving on a reef in Papua New Guinea when I came across a sea fan and swam up for a closer inspection. As I gazed at it I became aware, at some subliminal level, that there was more going on. I gazed more intently. Gradually I began to notice a few tiny, ghost-like shrimps *Periclimenes* sp. As I gazed across the sea fan, focusing at different points on it, I began to notice more and more of these transparent shrimps. Eventually I realized that there were dozens of them all over the fan. Presumably they were using it as a base from which to snatch passing organisms from the current. In this photograph I have counted six shrimps; perhaps there are more.

△ Some creatures of the reef will use the defences of another creature for their own protection. This curious little crab *Zebrida adamsi* is an example as it is only to be found clinging to the venom-packed spines of sea urchins. Here, a fire urchin *Asthenosoma* sp. plays host to such a crab. Little is currently known about the behaviour of the crab. It is fairly rare and does not seem to be found on solitary urchins but rather where several are present. Only one crab, however, is ever found on one urchin.

◁ While swimming along the sandy patches bordering a reef an observant diver is likely to come across a fascinating sight. Long, slender fish known as gobies are commonly spotted lying on the sea floor next to a burrow. A diver who watches from afar and does not scare the goby into the hole may well be rewarded by the sight of a small, scurrying shrimp that darts out of the hole, pushing or carrying a pile of coral rubble with its claws. It deposits the material beyond the entrance to the burrow and vanishes back down it again, only to reappear shortly, continuing in its Sisyphean toil. This is a pistol shrimp. Its poor eyesight has led it to develop a fascinating symbiotic relationship with the goby which acts as its look-out. The shrimp uses its long antennae to keep the goby in constant tactile contact. If danger approaches, the goby, followed by the shrimp, dives down the burrow and neither emerges until the threat has passed. The burrow, excavated by the untiring efforts of the shrimp, provides the goby with a secure hiding place in exposed areas of sand. This symbiotic relationship is termed mutualistic as both creatures benefit. Six years ago, while exploring the lagoon of Sanganeb atoll, I came across several familiar species of goby sharing burrows with pistol shrimps. Once, however, I spotted a tiny, dark shape paddling in a hovering position within a burrow. I could not make out what it was but I doubted it was a goby as it was not lying in a typical position at the entrance to the burrow. Six years later and an hour of waiting in front of such a burrow solved the mystery. A beautiful goby *Lotilia graciliosa*, considerably smaller and more timid than any I had seen before, eventually emerged with its partner shrimp *Alpheus rubrimaculata*. Note the dexterity of the shrimp: it is balancing a piece of coral rubble with its smaller pair of antennae, while simultaneously enfolding the goby within the longer pair.

△ The brightly banded boxer shrimp *Stenopus hispidus* makes a living by cleaning parasites from fish. As such, it leads a protected existence and does not expect to be gobbled by the very fish it serves. But how do the fish learn the rules? In the lagoon of Sanganeb atoll, I once came across a curious sight. A juvenile scorpionfish *Scorpaenopsis* sp. was trying to creep up on – and presumably eat – this boxer shrimp. Every time the scorpionfish crept within range, the shrimp would fasten a claw onto the lip of the little fish and start to pinch. The fish would writhe, retreat and start again. It was painful to watch the little scorpionfish receiving its education. Eventually, however, the fish would learn that it was a waste of time trying to eat a shrimp with this particular coloration; the possibility of the shrimp cleaning the fish would then be established.

◁ The murky lagoon waters between reef and shore provide a nursery area for many species of reef fish and a home for many other creatures. Off-shore from the Florida Keys is an immense lagoon of shallow water that gradually deepens. It is an area of turtle grass, gorgonian whip corals, occasional clumps of sponge and rare lumps of coral. The sponges are infested with worms, snails and shrimps, but they also provide shelter for some tiny reef juveniles. Here, a juvenile blue angelfish *Holacanthus bermudensis*, 2 centimetres (¾ of an inch) in length has taken refuge in the convolutions of a green sponge. It is investigating a tiny hermit crab – a crab that inhabits an abandoned mollusc shell – that is crawling across its sponge.

△ Only a few metres away from the blue angelfish, a juvenile grey angelfish *Pomacanthus arcuatus* of about 4 centimetres (1½ inches) in length hovers next to another sponge. Like the blue angelfish, it has a striped coloration to confuse predators. When the grey angelfish reaches about 20 centimetres (8 inches) in length it will school with others of its species in the lagoon, before moving on to the reef where it will join a mate with which it will live. The adult colour is a drab grey. During the course of several days investigation, this juvenile individual was encountered at different clumps of sponge and coral; the tiny blue angelfish, however, always remained with the same sponge.

Adult angelfish include some of the most spectacularly coloured of fish. Perhaps the most splendid of all is the queen angelfish *Holacanthus ciliaris* of western Atlantic reefs. Here we see two varieties of coloration: one is predominantly blue, the other mainly yellow. Queen angelfish are shy and difficult to approach. They tend to favour gloomy overhangs in the reef and are not always as easy to spot as their gaudy colours might suggest. A diver finding one and slowly pursuing it will discover that it flushes out other queen angelfish that race to challenge it as it moves into their territory. Following just one queen angelfish for a few minutes can therefore result in as many as a dozen retreating ahead of you where earlier you saw none. Queen angelfish, like many other angelfish, feed on sponges. An easier way to get a photograph of one is to find a sponge on which the local angelfish have been feeding, and wait patiently. Sooner or later they will arrive to feed. The white area of sponge beneath these fish is the area of tissue the fish have damaged as they feed.

◁ The Indo-Pacific emperor angelfish *Pomacanthus imperator* displays another example of the bizarre colour schemes adopted by the angelfish. Emperors are normally timid and difficult to approach. They can, however, be very aggressive towards rivals: I once watched three scratched and injured emperors remorselessly chasing each other through the narrow cracks in a coral head. While exploring a cave on a night dive off Sanganeb atoll, I was startled by a loud thumping noise right next to my ear. I nearly leaped out of my skin. Shining my torch in the direction from which the noise had come I found an emperor bedded down in a crack for the night. I could not work out how it had generated its auditory signal but I recognized it as a warning, took heed and left.

△ The royal angelfish *Pygoplites diacanthus* is one of the most common Indo-Pacific angelfish. This one was photographed on Osprey Reef off the Australian coast. Its strongly striped patterning obscures the body shape and is an example of disruptive coloration. Investigation into the eye structure of reef fish has shown they are rich in cone cells, which allow perception of colour, so the splendid colour schemes the fish have evolved are visible to the fish themselves. Stripes are often situated around the eyes to hide them. A dark spot, sometimes ringed with white, is often found near the tail, serving as a false eye. A predator will have trouble deciding where the fish's head is located. Colours and patterns also allow reef fish to recognize members of their own species on a crowded reef; and some fish are even able to vanish into their backgrounds by changing colour.

▽ Angelfish (family Pomacanthidae) are closely related to the equally beautiful butterflyfish (family Chaetodontidae). One distinguishing feature is the sharp, sabre-shaped protective spine on angelfish, extending back from the gill cover. Here, a tiny juvenile butterflyfish *Chaetodon ornatissimus* of about 3 centimetres (1 inch) in length hides among the corals of a Papuan reef. It is easy to see how its coloration allows it to blend into its background. Some juvenile butterflyfish mature on the reef while others grow up around the sponges or isolated coral heads of lagoons.

On reaching maturity, many species of butterflyfish form mated pairs for a marriage that often lasts for life. These two, photographed on Osprey reef, appear indistinguishable at first glance; but notice how the spots on the following fish that turn into bars on the upper rear of the body follow a different direction from those on the leading fish *Chaetodon pelewensis*. The following fish may be a hybrid between this species and the closely related *C. punctatofasciatus*. Several species of angelfish and butterflyfish can form hybrids; indeed one occasionally spots a hybrid butterflyfish with a hopelessly confused coloration. The hybrids are often capable of breeding so a sequence of variations can result. Note the battling corals behind the fish: the tall, pale *Acropora palifera* is being attacked by a pale purple *Montipora*. The dead area between the corals – where the *Acropora* has been killed – is clearly visible. ▷

▽ The crown butterflyfish *Chaetodon paucifasciatus* is one of the prettiest in the Red Sea. The problem for the photographer trying to photograph a pair of butterflyfish is that each fish is constantly swimming off in a different direction, especially at the approach of a diver. If they come together again, it is inevitably when they are safely out of photographic range. During the hours spent following pairs of these fish over Red Sea reefs I have learned something of their behaviour. They seem to have excellent eyesight: if they become separated, one will swim to the top of the nearest coral head and hover conspicuously until its mate comes over. Or perhaps it is not a question of vision: there may be a simple piece of instinctive behaviour at work. If a fish becomes separated from its mate, it swims to and waits at the nearest high coral head, so both will know where to find each other. Crown butterflyfish are aggressive towards other pairs of their species and will chase them out of their territory.

The fish of the reef that are encountered hovering in crevices during the day are usually nocturnal. This pair of masked butterflyfish *Chaetodon semilarvatus* from the Red Sea, is a good example. Most butterflyfish, however, are diurnal; at night they lie in hiding places and many species actually change colour, darkening themselves to blend with their surroundings. ▷

▽ A pair of banded butterflyfish *Chaetodon striatus* glides along a Bahamian reef in the western Atlantic. There are well over 100 known species of butterflyfish and not all are confined to coral reefs. Indeed, though they seem fragile, many species are very hardy: they can be found in what might appear to be the most unsalubrious of habitats, such as in the filthy waters of harbours.

The spotfin butterflyfish *Chaetodon ocellatus* is another species of butterflyfish commonly encountered on the reefs of the western Atlantic Ocean. The flattened disc-like shape not only allows it to move through narrow gaps of coral, but also to remain stable and not tilt from side to side when moving at slow speed. The butterflyfish of the reef enjoy a varied diet. Many feed on individual coral polyps so are constantly browsing: as soon as one polyp is plucked its colonial neighbours will withdraw and the butterflyfish has no choice but to move on. Other food items include small crustaceans and worms. The pyramid butterflyfish *Hemitaurichthys polylepsis* is unusual in that it forms large schools that feed on the zooplankton in the open water beyond the reef.

▷

◁ A pair of bannerfish *Heniochus chrysostomus* hovers in a crevice of soft corals on Osprey Reef, Australia. These graceful fish are closely related to the butterflyfish and angelfish. Bannerfish can be encountered in varying numbers: from solitary individuals and pairs to enormous schools. While I was diving the point of Shaab Rumi atoll in the Sudanese Red Sea, it was fascinating to watch groups of mating fish gather during the course of each afternoon. Among these would be a regular collection of the local species of bannerfish. They would invariably gather under the same coral overhang and be gone by the morning. Bannerfish feed by plucking bottom-dwelling invertebrates from the reef.

△ Although these exquisite Moorish idols *Zanclus cornutus* look as if they are close relatives of the bannerfish, they are in fact better understood as a variation on the surgeonfish design. The Moorish idol has an enormous distribution, stretching all the way from Africa, through the Indian and Pacific Oceans, to Mexico. Curiously, it is not found in the Red Sea. Its colossal range may be due to the slow larval and post-larval stages of development. After mating, the developing fish spends a great while drifting on open ocean currents before establishing itself on a reef. This pair was photographed on a reef in Papua New Guinea, feeding on the grey soft coral *Sinularia* sp. visible immediately behind the tail of the rear fish. The white patches are where the fish have removed tissue.

This school of orangespine unicornfish *Naso lituratus* only partly justifies its common name. The 'orangespine' refers to the pair of scalpel-like spines carried on each side of the body just before the tail. The bright orange colour that surrounds the spines is presumably to warn other fish of these weapons. The term 'unicorn' refers to the fact that other species of this genus have developed a horn that projects from the front of the head. Unicornfish belong to the surgeonfish family (Acanthuridae), all the members of which bear defensive spines at the base of the tail. At the crest of an Indo-Pacific reef, where the coral growth is stunted and the terrain is overgrown by mats of algae, a diver is likely to see brightly coloured surgeonfish. If the diver chooses to swim towards them – or rather towards those areas of algae – the surgeonfish will react aggressively to protect the algal mats on which they feed, swooping towards the diver before speeding past and preparing for another charge. Their spines provide them with effective weapons for slashing a rival. The unicornfish illustrated here are far more timid in temperament. They also feed on bottom-dwelling algae but do not actively cultivate and then fiercely defend it and are normally solitary and difficult to approach. I had just come across this group on a reef in the Egyptian Red Sea when a big, old, green turtle *Chelonia mydas* swam past in the background. I had to decide whether to stay with the unicornfish or pursue the turtle; the turtle won and took me on a merry trip down the reef, always staying just out of photographic range. When I returned to where the unicornfish had been, they had gone.

Many reef fish exhibit radically different colorations at different stages of growth. While a juvenile will be exclusively concerned with survival, an adult may well adopt a very different colour scheme that serves another function, such as signalling sexual maturity to attract a mate. One of the most spectacular colour changes occurs in the clown coris *Coris aygula*. This fish belongs to a large and often brightly coloured group called the wrasses (family Labridae). This tiny juvenile, about 4 centimetres (1½ inches) in length, was photographed over a patch of sand surrounded by dead coral in the lagoon of Shaab Rumi atoll in the Sudanese Red Sea. I spent many hours searching seemingly identical sand patches for further juvenile reef fish, but curiously I was successful only once; and on this patch I found not one, but three of these juveniles, as well as several other juvenile wrasses. It seemed as if they had chosen this small area as their nursery. The juvenile clown coris has two spectacular false eyes on the back half of its body. Two are more effective then one: they could confuse a predator into thinking it was seeing a much larger fish head-on, rather than a small fish from the side. I was photographing this fish at dusk; it began to slow its swimming pattern and make nodding gestures to a spot where a lump of coral rock met the sand. Suddenly it dived into the sand and vanished; it was bedtime.

This is a mature male clown coris of about 50 centimetres (20 inches) in length. By now the fish has little to fear from reef predators and is more concerned with establishing a territory by chasing away rival males and attracting females with which to mate. The dark colour and the bump on his forehead signal sexual maturity.

▽ Despite appearances to the contrary, these two little fourline wrasses *Larabicus quadrilineatus* are not greeting each other with affection. At about 4 centimetres (1½ inches) in length they bear the colouring of juveniles or females: mature males are larger, much darker and lose their stripes. I came across this spectacle in the lagoon of Shaab Rumi atoll in the Sudanese Red Sea. There were three of these little fish; two were continually squaring off against each other and freezing for several seconds in this posture. Then their mouths would interlock and a violent wriggling, twisting tussle would follow which could last a good 15 seconds. They would break off for perhaps a minute before repeating the procedure. The third fish always remained aloof in the background. It seems unlikely that they were competing for the third fish as none was a mature male. It is more likely that the battle was over territory.

As in so many walks of life, if there is someone willing to do some hard work then there is likely to be someone else more than willing to take advantage. Here, in the Egyptian Red Sea, a goatfish *Parupeneus forsskali* burrows in the sand in search of worms and crustaceans to eat. Under its chin, and now extended into the sand, are two sensory appendages known as barbels. When these manage to locate a food item, the goatfish will start to dig energetically, creating a cloud of displaced sand. Hovering just behind the goatfish and ready to snatch anything that it uncovers and misses, is a checkerboard wrasse *Halichoeres hortulanus*. The sharp canine teeth with which it impales small crustaceans are clearly visible. To attract the wrasses of a reef, a diver need only turn over a few stones or waft a hand over the sand. ▷

One of the most extraordinary fish of Indo-Pacific reefs is the cleaner wrasse *Labroides dimidiatus*. Various species of wrasse and juveniles of some other groups (such as certain angelfish), will act as cleaners for other fish: they will be allowed to feed unmolested on small, parasitic crustaceans that attach themselves to their 'clients'. They will also help themselves to gulps of mucus, but that is part of the price paid for the service. Cleaner fish will take up specific locations on the reef and await the arrival of other fish. Any fish that swims through the cleaner's domain is likely to be closely approached to see if it will stop and allow itself to be cleaned. Here, on an Egyptian reef, a wrasse *Thalassoma klunzingeri* swims through a cleaner station and is immediately approached by a cleaner fish.

The Red Sea houndfish *Tylosurus choram* hunts just below the surface. Its mouth is filled with needle-sharp teeth, perfectly designed for catching fish the size of the cleaner wrasse. The houndfish, however, must also visit the cleaning station. It will not descend to the level of the cleaner fish but finds a shallow cleaning station and then hovers directly above with mouth held open, signalling that it requires cleaning. The cleaner wrasses swim up to the houndfish and skirt across its body performing their task. Although houndfish can be spotted in considerable numbers just below the surface, it is almost impossible to get close enough to them for a photograph. It was only when I encountered this one being cleaned that I managed to get near enough to it to succeed.

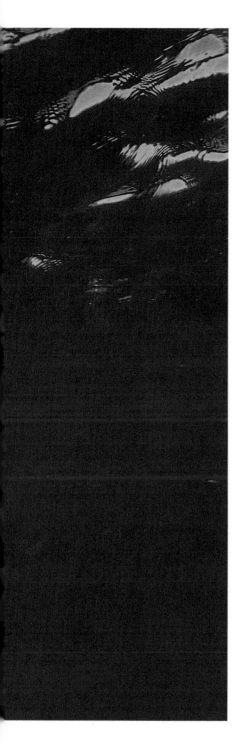

The mightiest predators of the reef become docile when being cleaned by cleaner wrasses. Sharks, tunas and groupers all allow the cleaner to perform its task in safety. Here, on a Red Sea reef, a giant moray eel *Gymnothorax javanicus* opens its mouth to allow cleaner fish inside. A second cleaner can just be made out as a faint blue line underneath the roof of the moray's mouth. The cleaner fish will skirt across the moray's body plucking at crustacean parasites and snatching bits of mucus along the way. The eel will then signal by opening its mouth wide that the cleaners may enter in safety. If the eel needs encouragement the cleaner fish will nudge at the corners of its mouth until it complies. Fish being serviced by cleaner wrasses often seem to go into a strange, passive, trance-like state during the process. Good underwater photographs of reef fish will usually reveal cleaner fish in attendance; this is very often the only time a photographer can get sufficiently near to the subject.

◁ The coloration of this pair of cleaner fish – white and blue with a broad, black stripe – warns other reef fish that its owners are not to be eaten, and so they are allowed to live unmolested on the reef. Although this wrasse is not found on the reefs of the western Atlantic, there is a goby *Gobiosoma oceanops* in this region that acts as a cleaner fish and has the same coloration. Presumably there were *Labroides dimidiatus* cleaner wrasses (or their similarly coloured ancestors) on these reefs long ago; at some stage they must have died out, but not before the local reef fish had learned that this coloration conferred a protected status. The goby that closely matched the colour of the cleaner fish filled the niche vacated by its demise.

◁ Given that the Indo-Pacific cleaner fish leads something of a charmed life on the reef, it is not altogether surprising that some other fish would attempt to mimic the cleaner wrasse and so share in its protection. At first glance these fish look like cleaner wrasses. But close inspection, particularly to compare the shape of the mouth to that of the fish in the previous photograph, reveals differences. These fish belong to the blenny family (Blenniidae) and are commonly known as false cleaners or mimic blennies *Aspidontus taeniatus*. Their mimicry skills are considerable. Normal blennies swim with a pronounced wriggling of the body while wrasses tend to pump their pectoral fins while keeping the body still. The mimic blenny swims like a wrasse. The cleaner wrasse will often signal its readiness to clean other fish by performing a special swimming pattern of bobbing up and down. Unabashed, the blenny performs the same. Reef fish not only mistake the mimic for the real thing and do not molest it, but they will also closely approach it expecting to be cleaned. The result is a nasty shock: the blenny rushes forward and bites a chunk out of the fooled fish before fleeing, with furious victim in hot pursuit. The blenny's mouth is a different shape to that of the cleaner wrasse because it hides long, needle-sharp teeth. The success of these mimics is inversely proportional to their population size in comparison to the real cleaner: the more there are fooling and biting fish, the sooner the true cleaner's special status would collapse and the whole system break down. So, not only are false cleaners difficult to distinguish from the real thing, they are also comparatively rare.

Although Caribbean reefs lack Indo-Pacific cleaner fish, several other fish will perform cleaning services. Here, on a Bahamian reef, this school of yellow-phase blueheads *Thalassoma bifasciatum*, a common species of wrasse, will perform the task. The common name derives from the fact that there are two colour variations within the species: this predominantly yellow version, and also the very different appearance of the large, so-called 'supermales' that have a blue head and no yellow in their coloration. The sea fan in this photograph was on the top of the highest clump of coral on the reef. The yellow-phase blueheads were swarming across it and presumably plucking tiny crustaceans off its surface. Beneath the sea fan and a few metres away was this stoplight parrotfish *Sparisoma viride*. The

blueheads swarmed over the sea fan in chaotic fashion and the parrotfish did not appear to notice them. Once in a while, however, they formed a dense, wriggling mass in the centre of the fan. The parrotfish reacted by swimming over to the coral head and then hovered in a head-up position just beneath the fan, announcing its desire to be cleaned. The blueheads approached in order to clean the parrotfish, and I closed in to get a photograph. My presence caused the parrotfish to retreat and the whole process started again. The parrotfish would swim over only when the yellow fish were swarming in their little ball of colour; set against the sea fan it was a conspicuous sight. Whether the blueheads were intentionally signalling their willingness to clean any clients is open to conjecture.

Parrotfish are closely related to wrasses and swim like them by pumping the pectoral fins, though a startled parrotfish will use its tail to accelerate away from danger. Parrotfish also have over-the-top colour schemes. The teeth are fused into a strong beak, which gives them their common name. Many parrotfish feed by scraping algae off coral rock. If the 'rock' happens to be a living coral colony then it will be damaged; scrape marks on coral are evidence of parrotfish feeding. In these cases algae, polyps, mucus and corallite are all swallowed. The corallite material passes through the body and is expelled as sand. Here, in the Red Sea, a male steepheaded parrotfish *Scarus gibbus* scrapes at coral rock. Note the Klunzinger's wrasse *Thalassoma klunzingeri* in attendance. ▷

△ The coloration of male and female parrotfish of the same species can vary considerably. Many species have two distinct adult colour phases: the initial phase, which is a fairly subdued overall green, red or brown, and a terminal phase, which is far more gaudy. The initial phase is exhibited by females and, in some species, males that will mate in groups with females. The terminal phase is seen only in larger, solitary males that mate individually with females. This mature female steepheaded parrotfish has, like the other diurnal fish of the reef, bedded down in her favourite hiding place for the night. Many parrotfish extrude a mucus envelope about themselves which traps their scent and prevents them from being detected by nocturnal hunters.

This is a terminal phase rusty parrotfish *Scarus ferrugineus* photographed in the Red Sea. Parrotfish occur in considerable numbers on the reef. Some feed individually, others in schools of many dozen. They affect the structure of the reef perhaps more than any other fish, as they can extensively damage coral colonies by scraping their surfaces while feeding. Such areas will then become vulnerable to infection and also to invasion by algae or other corals. One or two of the largest species will feed directly off the coral itself with obviously damaging results. Parrotfish are the 'sand factories' of the reef: they excrete the indigestible limestone coral rock as ground up granules. Despite the abundance of parrotfish on coral reefs, most species are wary of divers and difficult to approach. As with the vast majority of reef fish, the photographer must hope to find an individual parrotfish that is less timid than its fellows and then take as many pictures of it as possible.

It is mid-afternoon on this Red Sea reef and something strange is happening. The male parrotfish *Cetoscarus bicolor* have abandoned their usual activity of feeding among the corals and have taken up station in the current at the end of the reef. One of them can be seen *above*. They swim in circles with mouths gaping open. Every few moments one will stop circling and chase another male away as they establish territories. Some swim high up above the deeper corals, while others have taken up position at the shallow edge of the reef. Normally they are unapproachable and impossible to photograph. But now they are so engrossed with their ritual that they ignore me and I can get close.

I look back at the coral wall and see an amazing sight: a dozen females of the species are waiting just below the surface, looking out towards the males. The females are normally brown with a yellow stripe; but the stripes have all but vanished, a signal perhaps that they are ready to mate. The first sets off into the open water towards the males. One swims briskly up to her, mouth agape. She cuts him dead and continues on her route. Another approaches and is ignored. He returns, crestfallen, to his domain. Then another approaches and she allows him to swoop up next to her. They synchronize their swimming as can be seen *below*. Cheek to cheek they swim ever faster, up towards the surface and out away from the reef. They accelerate forwards, sides almost touching, and simultaneously release white clouds of eggs and sperm into the water. As they do so, they veer apart and create a vortex behind them of swirling gametes. The act is all but complete and the female returns to the reef wall. But a group of fish moves in to feed on the floating gametes. The male chases them off. Now the current will carry the fertilized eggs away to begin their development in the comparative safety of open water.

The largest of the parrotfish is the bumphead parrotfish *Bolbometopon muricatum* of Indo-Pacific reefs. Measured at up to 1.2 metres (4 feet) in length, it probably grows larger still. Bumphead parrotfish move across the reef in schools that can number dozens of fish. They feed in the same way as other parrotfish, by scraping at the surface of coral rock, but will also bite chunks out of the coral itself. They have even been observed using their bulbous heads to ram and break up coral before feeding on it. They are normally immensely wary and virtually impossible to approach. On one occasion while diving the northern point of Sanganeb atoll in the Red Sea, I spotted a school of bumphead parrotfish that did not immediately flee at my approach. They kept about 5 metres (16 feet) away – too far to photograph – but showed no signs of panic. A week later, while I was diving the same point again, I spotted a couple of bumpheads on top of the reef. For several minutes I swam parallel until they led me across the shallow reef flat to the rest of the school. Slowly I closed the gap. Every time the school looked as if it would flee I rushed off in pretended panic in the opposite direction, only to then sneak back. Finally I managed to get in among them and accompany them on their foraging. This is when the photograph was taken.

While the sandy areas of a reef lagoon cannot compete with the reef itself in terms of the variety or abundance of its animals, interesting creatures are to be encountered nevertheless. Many of the animals that live in this exposed area are coloured appropriately to blend with the sand. Many bury themselves beneath it to hide, or construct a burrow for protection against predators. The Moses sole *Pardachirus marmoratus* of the Red Sea is well camouflaged when at rest on the sand; it will also bury itself beneath it and become invisible. This sole, however, has another layer of defence: glands that secrete a bitter-tasting fluid that repels predators. Scientists investigating this fluid have discovered that it is even capable of repelling sharks. Analysis of the composition of the toxin revealed a chemical called pardaxin that dissolves fats: a fish that attempted to eat a Moses sole would suffer alarming consequences as the toxin would break up the oils in its gill membranes and disrupt their ability to function.

Numerous species of fish excavate burrows in the sand that provide them with protection. The yellowhead jawfish *Opisthognathus aurifrons*, occasionally encountered in the sandy areas bordering Caribbean reefs, is an example. A diver who chooses to leave the reef and swim over the sand would be well advised to move as slowly as possible, or the timid burrow-dwellers of the sand will hastily dart into their holes. The yellowhead jawfish feeds by hovering a little distance above its burrow and plucking organisms carried by the current. After mating, the male of the species incubates the eggs by carrying them in his mouth. When he wishes to feed, he will deposit them in the burrow; hunger sated, he takes them back into his mouth afterwards. Next to the jawfish is a large tube worm and numerous, smaller ones. These worms build protective tubes and their gills are modified into tentacular processes that filter food particles from the water. Tube worms have light-sensitive structures on their tentacles with which they sense changes in light intensity. They are also capable of sensing changes in water movement. A diver must move very carefully to get close to a tube worm as it will quickly vanish into its tube if it detects the presence of a diver. The larger tube worm in the picture probably belongs to the genus *Sabellastarte*.

The reef plays host to some of the most wonderfully coloured animals, and others that can instantly change colour to suit their background. The queen triggerfish *Balistes vetula* of western Atlantic reefs is often encountered on patchy areas of reef and sand where it adopts a pale overall colour to blend into the background. On a reef in the Bahamas I followed such a fish. Here (*above*) it has just reached the sheltering coral rocks and is pale in colour. A moment later (*right*) it has darkened to hide among the shadows of the reef. This queen triggerfish is pondering whether to dive into the crack in front of it, or continue swimming away. The term 'trigger' derives from the structure of the first dorsal fin, visible immediately above and just behind the eye. Note the large, stout first spine. There is a smaller spine behind it. An alarmed triggerfish will dive into a hole and jam itself by raising the first spine and then locking it in position with the second 'trigger' spine.

◁ The female titan triggerfish *Balistoides viridescens* is at her most fearless when guarding her egg mass. To begin the mating ritual, the female excavates a circular depression in the coral rubble and sand. She deposits her eggs in the centre of the depression and then coaxes a male to fertilize them, and then stands guard. Anything that comes too close will be charged and attacked: the triggerfish, armed with her strong, sharp, beak-like mouth, will often bite repeatedly. It is easy to overlook a drably coloured titan triggerfish and wander into her nest area. This individual from Sanganeb allowed me up close to photograph her and her egg mass (visible under her mouth) without, thankfully, launching an attack. It is not one of the experiences I am in a hurry to repeat.

△ This juvenile Picasso triggerfish *Rhinecanthus assasi* of about 3 centimetres (1¼ inches) in length has made its home in the lagoon of Sanganeb atoll in the Red Sea. It is about to dart into the safety of its hiding place. The floor of such lagoons is often mapped out by Picasso triggerfish varying in size from youngsters to 20-centimetre (8-inch) adults. The youngsters are easier to approach than the adults and it may be only the cautious that survive to maturity: the longer a fish hesitates before darting into its bolt hole the more likely it is to be caught by a predator. Picasso triggerfish defend their territories against each other with great hostility. A juvenile that does not dart into its hole but decides to swim off over the sand is in for a rough journey, as all the other Picasso triggerfish whose territories it encroaches will chase it away.

▽ The filefish are close relatives of the triggerfish and have a similar stout, erectable spine on the head. A filefish can erect its spine to intimidate a rival, jam itself in a hole (or the mouth of a predator that is attempting to swallow it), or even to make itself appear larger and more formidable than it actually is. This 3-centimetre (1-inch) filefish *Acreichthys tomentosus* photographed in Papuan waters, is in a quandary about the way in which to react to being photographed. By curving its tail and hovering nose down, it is trying to disguise itself. By raising its defensive spine, however, it is warning me that it is in fact a well-protected fish.

◁ The harlequin filefish *Oxymonacanthus longirostris* of Indo-West Pacific reefs have perhaps the strangest appearance of the filefish group. Adults are rarely over 5 centimetres (2 inches) long and usually travel in pairs, though here we have a trio. They are easily overlooked as they tend to hover very close to *Acropora* corals on which they feed by plucking at the polyps. The branches of the corals provide good protection against predators as the harlequin filefish will glide within the branches to hide itself as soon as it is threatened. Tiny juveniles of 2 centimetres (¾ of an inch) or less in length can sometimes be found hovering in a similar fashion among the fragile branches of *Seriatopora* corals, particularly in the murkier, more sheltered areas of a lagoon.

A Red Sea anemonefish *Amphiprion bicinctus* hovers next to its host anemone. The anemonefish, also known as clownfish, are members of a sub-group of the Indo-Pacific damselfish family. The anemonefish use the tentacles of sea anemones for protection. Indeed, so dependent are they upon their anemone hosts that they are never encountered in the wild without them. If a predator approaches, an anemonefish will retreat among the tentacles of its host; if it pursues the fish, the predator will get stung and will probably be captured by the anemone. It is thought that the mucus coat of the anemonefish protects it by impeding the firing of the anemone's stinging cells. When the threat has gone the anemonefish will hover near or above the anemone, feeding both on algae and zooplankton. Another advantage to the fish of this relationship is that the stinging cells of the anemone's tentacles may remove ectoparasites from the anemonefish. But does the anemone benefit from the presence of the fish in its tentacles? Certain butterflyfish feed on anemones and the anemonefish may well protect its host from such a threat. Several anemonefish can occupy a single anemone.

The coloration of this pufferfish *Arothron mappa* allows it to blend well with the background corals of a Papuan reef. A very poor swimmer, the pufferfish relies on several layers of defence. The skin is elastic and tough; in the related porcupinefish (family Diodontidae), it is covered in spines. The name pufferfish describes the ability of these fish to take in water, puff up and increase in size. In this way they are able to jam themselves into holes or avoid being swallowed by larger fish. Furthermore, pufferfish are immensely toxic, especially their liver and ovaries, and, to a varying extent, the skin, so it is not surprising that large pufferfish can be relatively unafraid of divers. Pufferfish meat is a gourmet delicacy in Japan, yet despite great care in the preparation of the fish, instances of poisoning and death still result.

Boxfish, also known as trunkfish (family Ostraciidae), are closely related to pufferfish. They have fused, bony plates that encase the body in a strong, protective box. Like their pufferfish cousins, they have developed a strong, toxic compound for their own protection, yet in the boxfish it can play a more active role as a startled boxfish will secrete the poison into the water. Many aquarium owners are aware of a stressed boxfish's ability to kill other fish in this way. The cowfish is a member of the boxfish family, identifiable by its horns. Here, a pair of honeycomb cowfish *Lactophrys polygonia* prepares to mate on a Bahamian reef. As the pair approached each other, one fish flushed bright yellow, the other bright blue. The significance of these colour displays is known only to the fish themselves.

Boxfish range well beyond the reef. They can instantaneously change colour, not only as part of their mating ritual but also for camouflage. Indeed, the first thing a boxfish will do when it sees a possible threat, such as a diver, is to blend with its background and hope it is not spotted. Here, on an expanse of sea-grass off the Florida Keys, a scrawled cowfish *Lactophrys quadricornis* attempts this technique. Once the fish realizes it has been seen it will swim off, simultaneously increasing the brightness of the blue scrawls in its coat to a spectacular iridescence. After swimming some distance in this conspicuous way the cowfish will suddenly appear to flick off the mains switch that governs the electric intensity of blue and glide into another hiding place. When you have been watching the most brightly coloured features of the fish, the sudden darkening of its colours will make it seem to vanish.

The crocodile flathead *Cociella crocodila* of the Indo-Pacific is an ambush predator that relies on its superb camouflage to remain unnoticed. It is well able to change colour to suit its background. Flatheads are typically encountered lying completely motionless on the sand or mud at the edge of the reef.

This individual was contentedly resting on the reef itself, the *Acropora* colony under its head providing a pillow, the colour which has been mimicked in the splotches of white adopted by the fish. Note the elaborate pattern of skin that has grown over the eye to obscure it and increase the animal's camouflage.

▽ When it comes to the active manipulation of coloration, few reef fish can compare with the trumpetfish (family Aulostomidae). With their vastly elongated bodies they hardly look like fish at all. Trumpetfish are cunning hunters of the smaller reef fish. Their success depends on their ability to hide, and to stalk and ambush other fish by constantly matching their background. A trumpetfish will hover at any angle that increases its concealment. I encountered this trumpetfish *Aulostomus chinensis* gliding towards me on a Papuan reef. As soon as it reached the sea fan it assumed the hue of its backdrop and hung at an angle intended to suggest that it was just another supportive branch of the fan.

On a Bahamian reef a Caribbean trumpetfish *Aulostomus maculatus* demonstrates another aspect of trumpetfish cunning. It is hunting some yellow-phase bluehead wrasses and has turned its head the same colour as its intended prey in the hope that they will confuse it for one of their own and allow it close enough to snatch one. The rest of its body is coloured to blend with the background. I was once diving a Bahamian reef when I spotted a school of yellow goatfish *Mulloidichthys martinicus* swimming rapidly in a highly agitated, circular formation like a wagon-train defending itself against rampaging Red Indians. I swam down to investigate. The enemy had infiltrated the circle: a trumpetfish was hovering in the centre. Protruding from its mouth was the tail of a goatfish. The whole head of the trumpetfish was vibrating under the desperate struggles of the doomed goatfish. Naturally I was out of film and missed a golden opportunity. ▷

Yet another hunting method in the trumpetfish's repertoire is to swim alongside another fish across the reef. In this way, it is obscured from potential prey. Sooner or later the covering fish will swim close to trumpetfish prey that does not spot the predator. One short dash and a meal is secured without the bother of having to spend ages stalking it. This method, however, is used sparingly by the trumpetfish to avoid teaching its prey to fear the approach of just about everything. Here a Caribbean trumpetfish has decided to hover in a cave just above a tiger grouper *Mycteroperca tigris*. It is daytime; the grouper is a predator that hunts at dusk, so reef fish will not now consider it a threat. A small fish that wanders close will probably see only the large grouper and therefore not flee. The trumpetfish is hovering at an angle that makes it virtually invisible to any fish that are within striking range.

Some of the reef's predators are so conspicuous that they specialize in hunting in the gaudiest parts of the reef where they blend more easily with their background. The lionfish *Pterois miles* of the Red Sea is an example. It is a member of a large family known as the scorpionfish (Scorpaenidae). In defence it is formidably armed: the anal, pelvic and dorsal fins are sharply pointed and coated in a venom capable of killing humans. The lionfish and its relatives should never be molested or handled by divers. Lionfish often occur in small groups; a diver who spots one and intends to photograph it should always check the surroundings very carefully as there are likely to be others nearby. Here, beneath a plate coral in the Egyptian Red Sea, a lionfish moves through some soft corals to stalk brightly coloured goldfish.

From straight ahead the lionfish looks like something from the metaphysical reaches of the human imagination. Its intended *Pseudanthias* prey is the blur of orange directly in front of the fish. The lionfish approaches its victim very slowly. With its fins splayed out among swirls of coral it looks like another invertebrate feature of the reef, perhaps most like a feather star. This lionfish, however, is hovering in the open water. Millimetre by millimetre it closes the gap on its prey which is fooled on two counts. Firstly, the object before it does not look like a fish. Secondly, it appears to be stationary. When the lionfish is close enough it will suddenly dart rapidly forwards; it will open its mouth wide and then unhinge it, thrusting it out ahead of its body to snatch the prey.

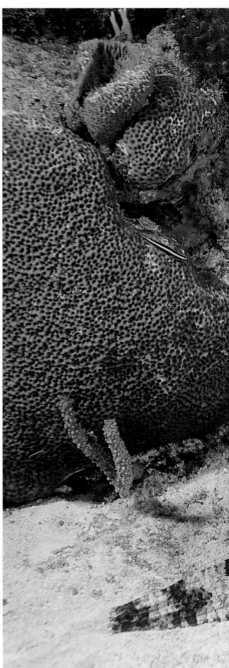

The scorpionfish family includes many members that have specialized in being inconspicuous. They will wait for a small fish or shrimp to wander within range and then dash forwards to engulf it. The venomous dorsal spines (as well as other spines in certain species) offer the fish considerable protection. The scorpionfish are often convinced they are invisible and secure in the knowledge that, should anything attack, their venomous defences will protect them. Once spotted by a diver, a scorpionfish can make a good photographic subject because it is in no hurry to move. Many species can rapidly take on the exact colours of their surroundings. This individual *Scorpaenopsis oxycephalus*, photographed on Sanganeb reef, waits like a mythical dragon in a medieval cave. Its body is covered in numerous, small outgrowths of skin that help to break up and obscure the animal's shape. Note the first dorsal fin spine that has been raised for protection.

A heavily camouflaged spotted scorpionfish *Scorpaena plumieri* from the Bahamas slithers along the sand. It is hoping to snatch one of the grunts in front of it. The yellow and silver fish are French grunts *Haemulon flavolineatum*; the paler fish with black bands on their rear backs are cottonwicks *H. melanurum*. Resting on the tan-coloured starlet coral *Siderastrea siderea* to the left of the scorpionfish are two small cleaner gobies *Gobiosoma genie*, one resting half way up the edge of the coral and a smaller one lower down, to the left of a tube sponge. They are waiting, in their typical posture, to clean parasites from any fish that happen to swim up. Perhaps the scorpionfish is hoping to snatch any grunt that approaches in order to be cleaned by the gobies.

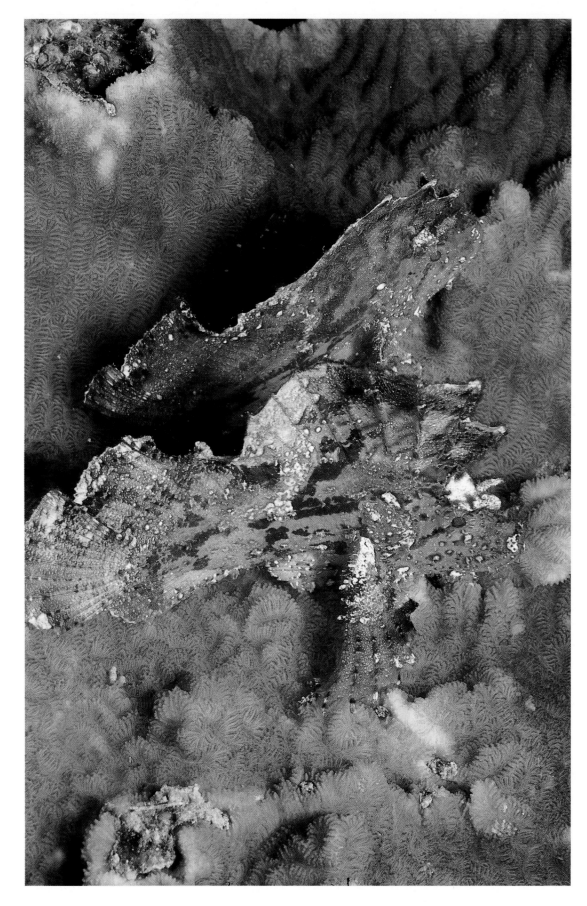

This pair of scorpionfish *Taenianotus triacanthus* photographed on a reef in Papua New Guinea demonstrates another example of scorpionfish mimicry. They are sometimes called leaf fish, and with good reason. Normally found in relatively shallow water, they gently rock their flattened bodies back and forth in the swell and look like small, swaying leaves or pieces of weed. A diver is unlikely to spot a leaf fish until one is pointed out to him, but then he will begin to see them for himself. Leaf fish will change colour to suit their backgrounds. There are so many variations on themes whereby the creatures of the reef manifest themselves that the level of awareness at which the diver spots something can be subliminal. I was once swimming over an area of coral rubble, barely glancing down at it, when suddenly something told me that I had seen a half-buried scorpionfish. I had not consciously seen it but, turning back and swimming to exactly the spot where my mind insisted that it was, I found it.

▽ Until 1980, Merlet's scorpionfish *Rhinopias aphanes* was known only from a single museum specimen. Then one day at the end of a dive on the Papuan reefs, Robert Halstead's wife Dinah mentioned to him that she had come across a curious creature that looked something like a scorpionfish. Robert photographed the fish, only the second Merlet's scorpionfish ever to be recorded. The Halsteads have since perfected the art of finding these astonishing scorpionfish. How often had I pestered them to find me one! It seems this fish favours the edges of profuse reefs that drop off to deep water. Once I was diving such a reef with Robert when I heard a muffled shout and saw him gesticulating at me. I swam over, hoping he had found an elusive *Rhinopias*. He pointed into a crevice and I gazed in. Nothing; just a clump of weeds and some feather stars. I shrugged. He pointed again at the same spot. I was getting irritated but looked more closely; the clump of weed had an eye. It had two eyes. It was a Merlet's scorpionfish.

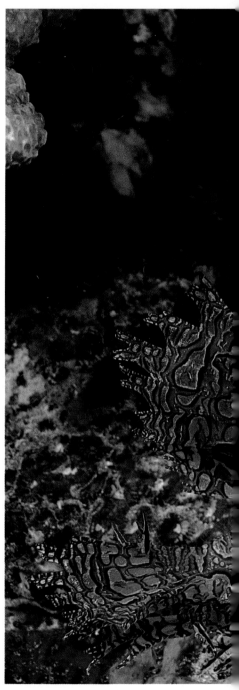

Only when a Merlet's scorpionfish is viewed from the side is it vaguely recognizable as a fish. Little wonder that this species has so long been overlooked by divers. From every other angle it appears to be a drab clump of weed. Merlet's scorpionfish is found in a variety of colours; some ▷ individuals are black with splodges of yellow and resemble feather stars. Indeed, when Robert and Dinah Halstead are looking for a Merlet's scorpionfish, they hunt for feather stars and then look more closely.

Scuttling across a Papuan reef is another extraordinary scorpionfish. This one *Dendrochirus biocellatus* is nocturnal. It is all of 4 centimetres (1½ inches) in length and does not swim like most fish but scurries across the bottom using the rays (supportive rods) of its pelvic fins like little legs; indeed it looks more like a crustacean. On its dorsal fin are two false eyes; the fin is angled so that the eyes are presented as a pair and intended to confuse me as to which end is which. The splayed-out pectoral fins serve to make the fish appear larger than it is. These scorpionfish are always in a hurry; if one darts into a hiding place you only have to turn off your torch for a second or two and it will invariably scurry out and continue on its quizzical way. The fin spines are probably highly venomous.

Every camouflage technique seen so far fades into insignificance when compared with the ability of the dreaded stonefish of the Indo-Pacific to vanish into its background. Illustrated here is a reef stonefish *Synanceia verrucosa* in the shallow lagoon of Sanganeb atoll. Unlike most scorpionfish whose spines are coated in toxic mucus, the dorsal spines of the related stonefish are grooved, and each groove leads to a sac of venom. If someone is unfortunate enough to tread on a stonefish the venom will be injected as if via a hypodermic needle and the result can be fatal. The best treatment for any injury inflicted by a stonefish or other member of the scorpionfish family, is to immerse the infected area of the body in water as hot as the victim can tolerate for at least an hour; the heat serves to break down the venom. Stonefish can bury themselves in the sand as shown here, or sit out in the open on the reef, and still be invisible.

▽ This stonefish, half buried in rubble, is all but impossible to spot. It is lying immediately behind the large rock that fills most of the right-hand side of this picture. Behind the apex of the rock is the dorsal fin of the fish. Follow this along to the left and one discovers a small, beady eye and then the vertical plunge of the mouth, distinguishing features for the species. Trying to find a stonefish is a miserable task. Before I had any stonefish pictures I used to spend fruitless hours searching in the lagoon at Sanganeb. On one particular trip, after many frustrating days, one of the resident lighthouse keepers asked me what I was forever searching for. When I told him he laughed and immediately pointed this one out from the shore. It was in water of a depth of only 30 centimetres (1 foot).

Some fish exist only on coral reefs while others, though not confined to the reef, are successful hunters of reef fish and commonly encountered there. Examples include various species of shark and also the large family of predatory jacks (Carangidae). There are numerous species and they vary in size from 50 centimetres (20 inches) in length to the mighty amberjack *Seriola dumerili* that can reach more than 1.5 metres (5 feet). The jacks are powerful and swift hunters of open water and usually predominantly silver in colour, though large individuals can take on a sinister, dark hue. These powerful, stately fish can be an impressive, and occasionally alarming sight underwater. On one occasion, while exploring undived reefs in Papua New Guinea, I was the first in the water and, setting off down the reef slope, I spotted a heavyweight, black shape charging towards me. At the last moment it changed direction and sped off into the distance. I just had time to identify it as a huge, old jack, blackened with age. Evidently it had never seen a diver before, and judging by the direction and speed with which it had vanished, it was unlikely to see one again. Jacks are often to be seen on the reef; some species form dense schools, others hunt in small squadrons, speeding just above the surface of the coral to snatch any unwary or sluggish fish that they might come across. Here, on the deep edge of Sanganeb reef, a pair of orange-spotted jacks *Carangoides bajad* swoops past a coral head to test the fitness of its population of schooling goldfish. The goldfish collectively dart for cover among the soft corals, and any stragglers would soon have fallen victim to the lightning jacks.

▷

This is a group of goldfish *Pseudanthias squamipinnis*. *Pseudanthias* are members of the grouper family (Serranidae) and, typical of the group, are protogynous: they begin life as females before finally maturing as males. The larger, purple-coloured fish with an elongated dorsal fin spine in the centre of the photograph is a mature male among the orange females. At the bottom is a fish in the process of changing from female to male. Typically, females considerably outnumber males: scientists studying *Pseudanthias* on coral heads in the Gulf of Eilat in the northern Red Sea found that, on average, there were eight females to every male. The males tend to be some distance apart from each other. They mate with the local females and, in effect, operate a harem system. If the male of such a group is removed then the largest female will change into a male. Evidently the very presence of a male among females inhibits their sexual metamorphosis. When trying to photograph *Pseudanthias*, one soon learns that the males are far more timid than the females. Both sexes will retreat into hiding places when a diver approaches; but the males are the first to hide and the last to emerge. It is not obvious why protogyny evolved; if an animal can produce female gametes more effectively at one size and male gametes at another, then the beginning of an answer may be at hand. There are, however, other unanswered questions. While diving Egyptian reefs I have occasionally encountered areas where hundreds of mature male *Pseudanthias* were to be found with not a female in sight.

The Indo-Pacific coral grouper *Cephalopholis miniata* is one of the most splendidly coloured members of its family. As it is an active hunter, it is difficult to understand how so conspicuous a coloration could help it to sneak up on prey. The answer seems to lie in the habitats where these fish are found: namely, in areas of the reef visited by strong currents. Brightly coloured soft corals, sea fans and feather stars abound in such areas and the coral grouper normally blends into the shadows of these flamboyant settings to hunt swarms of little planktivorous fish. There will often be several groupers ploughing, mouths agape, through such aggregations. I once came across a typical, current-bathed recess on a Papuan reef, jammed full of tiny fish seeking shelter. Hovering nearby was a coral grouper. It had its eye on the little fish but, because they were jammed into a sharply-lined crevice, was not keen to charge in after them and scratch itself on the coral wall. As I closed in to photograph the fish, a few moved out of their shelter to avoid me, only to fall victim to the coral grouper. I backed off and the coral grouper waited impatiently for me to continue my efforts so that he could feed.

The lunartail grouper *Variola louti* is another spectacular hunter of Indo-Pacific reefs. Groupers are usually encountered during the day hovering just above the reef floor or briskly skimming the coral wall as they search for food (*above*). The predatory repertoire of groupers begins with a highly developed sense of smell. Here, on an Egyptian reef (*right*), a cunning lunartail hovers in the current swooping up a coral cleft. He holds his position by lazily working his tail. The current carries the smells of the reef with it; if the lunartail grouper smells a potential meal he will swim up-current towards its source. On one occasion, while struggling through the murky lagoon entrance of an Egyptian reef, I encountered a pair of enormous old groupers hovering out in the open. They had positioned themselves in the centre of the current and were waiting to snatch any injured fish that it carried towards them.

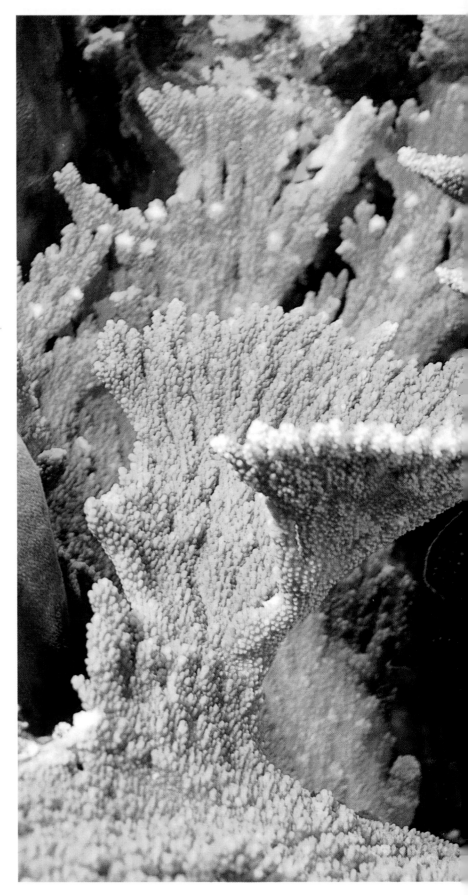

With a basically dark coloration and a body shape broken up by small, bright spots, the peacock grouper *Cephalopholis argus* is typically encountered in shady areas of the reefs throughout the Indo-Pacific. The species is usually timid and difficult to approach. Here, on a Papuan reef, two peacock groupers had been squabbling over which of them was to use this hiding place for shelter. After a few minutes of chasing, this fish backed victoriously into the overhang. Now that it had won the hiding place, it was in no hurry to retreat from it.

This pair of roving groupers (*Plectropomus pessuliferus*) has adopted a light-brown patterning to match the corals; the pale-blue dots and dashes have an uncanny resemblance to the blue water background. Roving groupers often hover over the sand at the edge of the reef as these two were doing when I first spotted them. They swam away at my approach so I moved into a hiding place and waited. Eventually curiosity overcame them and they followed me to investigate. While diving on the wall of Sanganeb reef, I once spotted a school of 100 roving groupers moving down the reef *en masse*. They were swimming towards the south-west point, where just about everything seems to mass for mating. Presumably it was their turn. Areas of reef swept by current are favoured haunts for groupers. The point to which this school was heading is populated by dozens of brownmarbled groupers *Epinephelus fuscoguttatus*. Their bulk, however, belies their timidity as they will flee at the approach of a diver.

Cardinalfish (family Apogonidae) come in a variety of colours, though the common name derives from those bright orange varieties that resemble officers of the papacy. Individuals of the silver species seen here are collectively known as glassfish by divers. These small plankton-feeders are nocturnal in their habits. During the day, they shelter in cracks and caves of the reef in schools that number many thousands. Year after year the glassfish occupy the same locations on the reef. The most numerous collections of glassfish I have ever seen were on the reefs of the Egyptian Red Sea; indeed, there was hardly a reef without several such schools in attendance. These vast swarms are an unavoidable temptation to local groupers: all day long different groupers will visit the cracks filled with glassfish and speed through them, mouths agape. The redmouth grouper *Aethaloperca rogaa* has a black overall colour and rarely ventures into the open, normally hiding in the darkest recesses of caves and cracks. The schools of glassfish that fill such unlit crevices are slowly whittled down by these unseen hunters. Here, hunger sated, such a grouper leaves his domain and the glassfish around him part in alarm.

This photograph was very nearly the last I ever took. A group of us had just been diving Sanganeb atoll. Below on the point were half a dozen grey reef sharks. As usual, their behaviour during the dive had been impeccable. Over the years I thought I had learned something about how to treat these animals. I had often swum along the surface far above them and they had never shown the slightest interest, never deviating from their trance-like patrols. On this occasion I had just clambered back into the inflatable boat when I spotted a trio of bottlenose dolphins *Tursiops truncatus* cruising on the surface. I grabbed a camera and set off on an interception course. I glanced down to the bottom and could see the sharks below, cruising over the sand. Then a vague shadow appeared on the surface: it was one of the dolphins, beginning to swim away. I knew I had to make it come back, so I went into my 'crazy dolphin' routine. I started squeaking and bleating through my snorkel and doing loop-the-loops and somersaults on the surface. It had the desired effect: the dolphins swam up for a closer look at this daft and clumsy version of themselves. I took a picture, then glanced back down to the reef. Curiously, all of the sharks were directly below looking up towards the surface. Then one, quickly followed by the rest, sped up from the bottom straight towards me. In a moment they were upon me. I just had time to kick one with my fin as I felt another bump my other leg and then brush it with its snout. For a couple of seconds I was surrounded by a swirling blur of sleek, copper-coloured forms. But the encounter ended as suddenly as it had begun: the sharks streaked, as a group, back down to the reef. Needless to say, the dolphins had also gone. Later, I mused on the mistakes I had made. Firstly, the sharks had encountered me on the surface, not on the reef. I knew from past experiences that such a sighting could make their behaviour radically more aggressive. Furthermore, on this occasion I had been giving off all the signals of an injured animal.

A school of bottlenose dolphins speeds through the lagoon of a Red Sea reef. Bottlenose dolphins often feed in shallow water on a wide variety of fish and invertebrates. A coral reef and the sandy shallows of its lagoon provide a rich source of such food. On another occasion I had an even closer encounter with a school of bottlenose dolphins when the water was crystal clear. After a dive I was snorkelling – *sans* camera – over to the anchor to release it from the bottom. A single bottlenose dolphin appeared and then, having ascertained that I had no camera, gleefully brought a school of 30 others in a stately procession directly in front of me. I shook my fist at them in frustration and they seemed to wave back. I am not an expert at translating dolphin-squeak into English, but their laughter is unmistakable.

The hawksbill turtle *Eretmochelys imbricata* is found on coral reefs world-wide, where it feeds on sponges. Hawksbills are very timid and usually to be seen streaking away from a diver. Robert Halstead has developed a technique for getting close and, unlikely as it sounds, it works. If you spot a hawksbill resting on the bottom you must not look at it or it will panic and flee. Approach it, very slowly, from the side pretending all the while not to know it is there. Then settle down next to it, still resisting the temptation to look at it. After perhaps 20 seconds look towards it. The turtle will be staring at you with a baffled expression. Immediately look away as if you find it thoroughly uninteresting. Half a minute later look again; it will still be staring at you, perhaps with a slightly hurt expression in its eyes. Look away again after a couple of seconds. By now the turtle will be getting thoroughly offended. Look again for a few seconds as if you are beginning to find it of interest, but then change your mind and look away. This the turtle cannot tolerate. It will leave the bottom and start swimming around you, determined to make you pay attention. Now is the time to get photographs, as I did here on a Papuan reef. I should add, however, that I was worried about the mental health of this particular individual. When I first spotted it on a Papuan reef it looked suspiciously as if it was trying to mate with the boat's anchor.

A green turtle *Chelonia mydas* swims across a Papuan reef. This species grows much larger than the hawksbill, reaching a shell length of 1.2 metres (4 feet) and a weight of more than 145 kilogrammes (320 pounds). The green turtle is a vegetarian and feeds on pastures of sea-grass. Sea turtles can dive to impressive depths. I once saw a loggerhead turtle *Caretta caretta* at a depth of 55 metres (180 feet) in the Bahamas. The turtle swam up from far below, had a look at me, and then set off back down along the reef. Every species of sea turtle is endangered as uncountable numbers are trapped and drowned in fishing nets. There are moves afoot to force the obdurate shrimp fishermen of the Gulf of Mexico's waters to install special escape hatches known as TEDs (Turtle Extruder Devices) in their nets. This is part of a desperate programme to ensure the survival of the world's most endangered sea turtle, the Kemp's ridley *Lepidochelys kempi*. With their eggs and flesh prized for food, their nesting beaches destroyed by tourist developments and their shells and carcasses used for ornaments, the future for the world's sea turtle populations looks bleak.

Of all the strange creatures I have encountered underwater, perhaps this bowmouth guitarfish *Rhina ancylostoma* is the most odd. This is a cartilaginous fish, and a variety of bottom-dwelling ray that seems to secretly want to turn into a shark. While resting on the bottom, guitarfish look like rays; but while freely swimming in open water, they more closely resemble sharks. The gills of the guitarfish are located on the underside of the body, like a ray, as opposed to the side of the body, like a shark. The bowmouth guitarfish feeds mainly on shellfish. Visible along the upper ridge of the head are wart-like growths. These are very enlarged denticles, the scales that make up the skin of cartilaginous fish.

Most people's idea of a shark is a swift and streamlined hunter, but sharks come in great variety. Around the coasts of Australia and Papua New Guinea is a group of sharks known as the wobbegongs that uses camouflage in order to ambush its prey. Here a tassled wobbegong *Eucrossorhinus dasypogon* of about 2 metres (6½ feet) in length takes up a typical posture on a Papuan reef: it lies, almost invisible, in a cave. Around the head is a heavy drapery of skin flaps, designed to obscure the head and so aid in concealment, a common technique among other bottom-dwelling ambushers, such as scorpionfish. Wobbegongs will leave their daytime hiding places at dusk and hunt for small fish during the night.

The whitetip reef shark *Triaenodon obesus* is one of the most commonly seen sharks of Indo-Pacific reefs. During the day it is often to be spotted resting on the sand or in caves before swimming lazily off at the approach of a diver. These sharks rarely reach 2 metres (6½ feet) in length, and most are considerably shorter. They are not considered dangerous to humans, though they can be pugnacious and persistent in the presence of dead fish. Here, on the wall of Osprey Reef beyond the Great Barrier Reef, a whitetip is hunting out some dead fish I had hidden in a hole. All was going well until I looked into the gloom beyond the reef and saw a solid wall of other sharks attracted to the smell of the dead fish bait. I was pondering my options, to panic or flee, when a big, old grouper came powering down the reef. He cast what appeared to be a contemptuous look at the horde of sharks posing threateningly in the background, grabbed the dead fish and swam off along the reef in triumph. With the smell of the dead fish gone the sharks soon disappeared.

The other most commonly sighted shark on Indo-Pacific reefs is the grey reef shark. Although it is not much longer than the whitetip, it is usually much more heavily built. The whitetip hunts and hides among corals; the grey reef patrols and hunts in the open water above the reef. This one was photographed on the south-west point of Sanganeb. The same grey reef sharks that ignore you in some circumstances can react violently in others, especially if they encounter you off the reef, or on the surface. Imagine the following situation: a diver is on a reef where a strong current is flowing. The grey reef sharks ignore him. He then gets swept off the reef and is unable to get back to it. In these circumstances any grey reef sharks that turn up now may well be far more interested in the diver than he would have expected. There is a school of thought that claims that open-water species of shark tend to be much bolder than their reef cousins when they come across a potential meal. It may in fact be the case that on venturing into open water, many sharks change their behaviour accordingly. On one occasion, while diving a deep reef in Papua New Guinea, I saw something of the simple efficiency of grey reef shark hunting methods. I was perched in a crack trying to photograph some schooling fish near the coral wall. I had been holding my breath for some time to avoid alarming them and betraying my presence with the bubbles from my breathing apparatus. Suddenly, the fish were all jammed up against the coral wall. Half a dozen grey reef sharks had come in from the open water and herded them up in order to feed. When they saw me, however, the sharks retreated.

The Arabic fishermen of the Red Sea call the silvertip shark 'Birigiya', the shining one, with good reason: the body shimmers in pale hues of platinum and bronze, and the back edges of the fins are coated in iridescent silver. No diver should be forgiven for confusing this bulky yet streamlined, muscle-packed yet graceful hunter for the skinny, weasel-like whitetip reef shark. Silvertips make the other reef sharks appear drab, clumsy and puny. The maximum recorded length of this species *Carcharhinus albimarginatus* is 3 metres (10 feet). This one is about 2.6 metres (8½ feet) long. However, Captain Abdul Nebi, a life-long fisherman of Red Sea waters, tells me that he has measured a captured silvertip at a colossal length of 4.2 metres (14 feet). According to him, silvertips are seasonal visitors to the Red Sea: they follow and feed off schools of migrating tuna. Any shark capable of preying on tuna must be able to produce dazzling bursts of speed, and this Abdul Nebi confirms. He explains that when fishermen spot a silvertip they must move to another location: they will never get a hooked fish back to the boat before the silvertip snatches it. The same is not true of the other sharks they encounter while fishing. Note the deep cut on the chin of this shark. Perhaps it had eaten a stingray and this was the injury inflicted by its barb. Silvertips are usually seen by divers on the deeper edges of Indo-Pacific reefs.

◁ Beyond the depth where stony corals can survive, the reef wall is studded with soft corals and daisy corals. Schools of planktivorous fish feed beyond the wall. In the foreground are yellow damselfish *Chromis analis*. Behind them, with brown heads and yellow-cornered white bodies, is a school of pyramid butterflyfish *Hemitaurichthys polylepsis*. The scuba diver cannot dive much further down than 50 metres (165 feet). Beyond that, the nitrogen in the air he breathes under pressure becomes narcotic. Any deeper and the oxygen on which his life depends becomes spontaneously toxic. Added to these barriers is the fact that the deeper he goes, the shorter time he can stay if he is to avoid decompression sickness (the bends). It is fortunate indeed that the greatest wealth of the reef is in its first 20 metres (65 feet). But as the stony corals become stunted and then vanish at greater depths, so other creatures come into dominance. What diver, on reaching his maximum depth on a deep dive, has not felt his sobriety lulled by the balm of narcosis? Gazing down into the beckoning, darkening unknown, most such divers would be tempted to continue. Perhaps future advances in diving equipment and breathing gases will allow sports divers to venture far deeper than they can now. No doubt they will be rewarded with new discoveries. But they will also have entered a domain patrolled by larger, more dangerous sharks, such as the tiger shark *Galeocerdo cuvier*.

Overleaf
Fifty metres (165 feet) down off the south-west point of Sanganeb Reef in the Sudanese Red Sea, some immature scalloped hammerheads *Sphyrna lewini* swim up to me for a closer look. They had approached from among a school of perhaps 100 small hammerheads. Their curiosity soon exhausted, the young sharks faded back into the gloomy background. Such schools – some comprising only juveniles, others only mature females, others a hotchpotch of both with a few mature males thrown in for good measure – are being discovered world-wide by divers as they explore the deeper reaches of remote reefs. Though scientists are debating the significance of this schooling behaviour, fishermen are not. A school of sharks is an all too tempting catch, and there are no regulations to prevent fishermen from removing these sharks, entire populations at a time.

A grey reef shark patrols its domain. The creatures of the reef have adapted and evolved over millions of years to live in this complex and dynamic habitat. They are now, however, ▷ vulnerable to the ability of Humankind to destroy it all in a matter of decades.

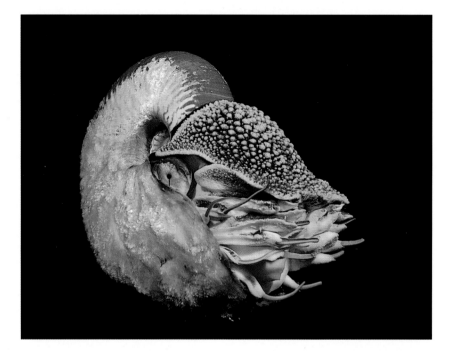

△ This, the rarest species of *Nautilus (N. scrobiculatus)*, is found in the depths beyond a few island groups off Papua New Guinea. *Nautilus* species are distantly related to the octopus and squid. They have an impressive ancestry originating some 450 million years ago when they were the first large predators of prehistoric seas. The geographical fossil record tells us that the ancestors of modern *Nautilus* barely survived a catastrophic decline in populations some 200 million years ago. Now there are only five surviving species which are often referred to as living fossils. This individual was caught in a baited trap at a depth of 200 metres (660 feet), far beyond the reach of a diver. It may be that, in the geological past, the ancestors of the modern *Nautilus* group inhabited the shallows. Then, as larger, swifter and more powerful predators (including the bony fish) evolved, the nautiloids were unable to compete in the rich shallows of the seas. They were pushed deeper and deeper down the reef wall to avoid predation. They are carnivores – scavenging on dead fish – but also capable of preying on crustaceans, such as lobsters and crabs. In some parts of the Pacific, they will come up onto the reef at night to feed before returning to the depths before dawn. The shell of *N. scrobiculatus* is covered in a velvety material known as the periostracum. It may serve to deter ectoparasites from settling as well as to act as a protective buffer against collisions with rocks. *Nautilus* swim rapidly backward by pumping water out of a tube known as the hypnome. They cannot see where they are going.

A
DIVER'S GUIDE
TO
CORAL REEF FISH

If you are a novice diver, the task of identifying the bewildering variety of fish on the reef may seem daunting. Reef fish identification books are of formidable bulk: finding a particular fish in the endless labyrinth of pages must seem a hopeless task. You might see a striking fish on the reef and try to remember its coloration. Perhaps it had a purple body, a yellow head and red stripes. In all likelihood, by the time you surface, you may well be insisting that the fish in question had a yellow body, purple stripes and a red head. Little wonder that identification can be fraught with difficulty!

The only sensible starting point is to be able to place each fish in a particular family, such as the parrotfish or butterflyfish families, by recognizing similarities in its overall body shape to other members of that family. Once this has been done, a survey in a specialist identi-fication book (such as those listed in the Further Reading section on page 194) should rapidly yield if not the definite answer, then at least an educated guess to the species in question.

Browsing through the various photographs in Part Two of this book will give you a degree of familiarity with the broad appearance of certain families of reef fish. For ease of reference, what follows here is a series of outline diagrams of the typical body shapes of the families you are most likely to encounter on coral reefs. Inevitably there are exceptions to the rule, as well as other reef fish not included here. But if this guide fires your interest so that you decide to investigate reef fish identification in greater detail, it will have served its purpose.

◁ There are often variations in body shape within families of reef fish. Here, a longer-nosed butterflyfish *Forcipiger longirostris* from the Pacific demonstrates such an adaption in the considerable elongation of its snout. To a biologist, form and function are inescapably entwined. This butterflyfish feeds on small invertebrates so the long snout is obviously a vital tool for plucking them from the most inaccessible of hiding places. Furthermore, because the eyes are positioned well back from the mouth, they are safe from anything encountered by the mouth that is potentially harmful. This longer-nosed butterflyfish has spotted something beneath a clump of coral festooned with crinoids.

A Diver's Guide to Coral Reef Fish

Reef fish families vary considerably in size. Where I refer to the size of a fish, very large means longer than 1m (3ft); large means longer than 60cms (2ft); medium means longer than 30cms (1ft); small means shorter than 30cms (1ft); and very small means less than 5cms (2ins). All of the families *below* are found on reefs world-wide, unless otherwise stated.

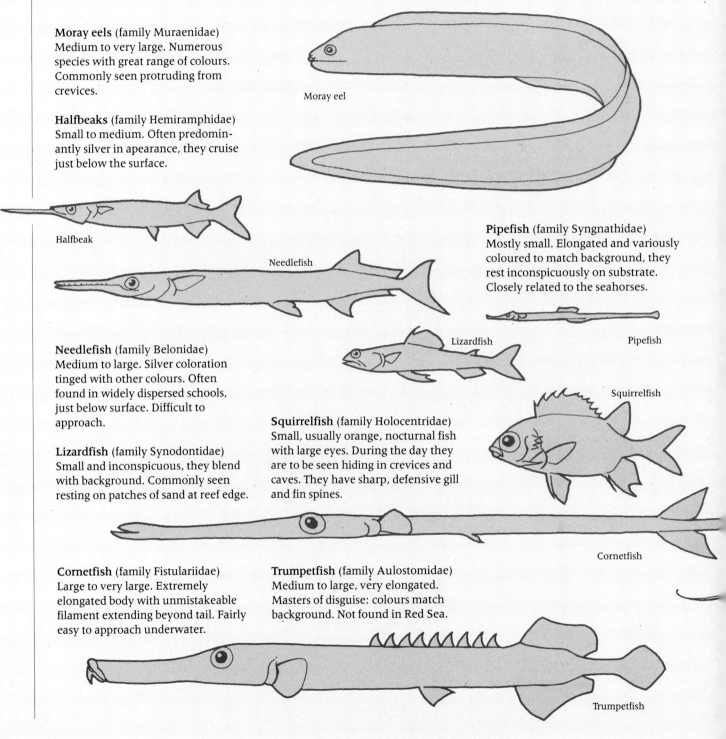

Moray eels (family Muraenidae) Medium to very large. Numerous species with great range of colours. Commonly seen protruding from crevices.

Halfbeaks (family Hemiramphidae) Small to medium. Often predominantly silver in apearance, they cruise just below the surface.

Moray eel

Halfbeak

Needlefish

Pipefish (family Syngnathidae) Mostly small. Elongated and variously coloured to match background, they rest inconspicuously on substrate. Closely related to the seahorses.

Lizardfish

Pipefish

Needlefish (family Belonidae) Medium to large. Silver coloration tinged with other colours. Often found in widely dispersed schools, just below surface. Difficult to approach.

Lizardfish (family Synodontidae) Small and inconspicuous, they blend with background. Commonly seen resting on patches of sand at reef edge.

Squirrelfish (family Holocentridae) Small, usually orange, nocturnal fish with large eyes. During the day they are to be seen hiding in crevices and caves. They have sharp, defensive gill and fin spines.

Squirrelfish

Cornetfish

Cornetfish (family Fistulariidae) Large to very large. Extremely elongated body with unmistakeable filament extending beyond tail. Fairly easy to approach underwater.

Trumpetfish (family Aulostomidae) Medium to large, very elongated. Masters of disguise: colours match background. Not found in Red Sea.

Trumpetfish

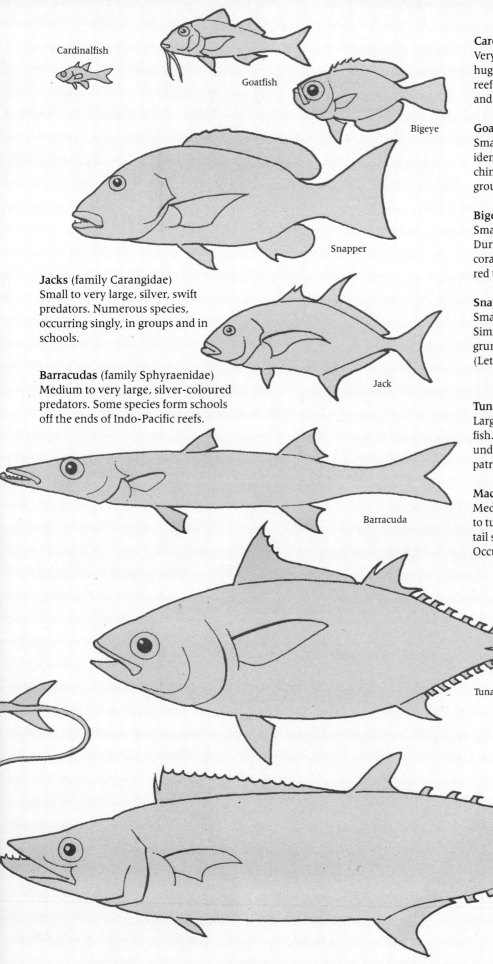

Cardinalfish

Goatfish

Bigeye

Snapper

Jacks (family Carangidae)
Small to very large, silver, swift predators. Numerous species, occurring singly, in groups and in schools.

Barracudas (family Sphyraenidae)
Medium to very large, silver-coloured predators. Some species form schools off the ends of Indo-Pacific reefs.

Jack

Barracuda

Tuna

Mackerel

Cardinalfish (family Apogonidae)
Very small fish that often occur in huge schools of mixed species on the reef. Colours include red, grey, silver and numerous striped patterns.

Goatfish (family Mullidae)
Small, variously coloured fish identified by pair of barbels on the chin. They swim in small, foraging groups or in large schools.

Bigeyes (family Priacanthidae)
Small, nocturnal fish with large eyes. During the day usually hidden under coral canopies. Colours range from red through to dull copper and grey.

Snappers (family Lutjanidae)
Small to large. Numerous species. Similar-looking families include the grunts (Haemulidae), emperors (Lethrinidae) and porgies (Sparidae).

Tunas (family Scombridae)
Large to very large, swift, predatory fish. Appear predominantly silver underwater. Occasionally seen patrolling in blue water beyond reef.

Mackerels (family Scombridae)
Medium to very large. Closely related to tunas, sharing same symmetrical tail shape and overall silver colour. Occur singly, in groups or in schools.

189

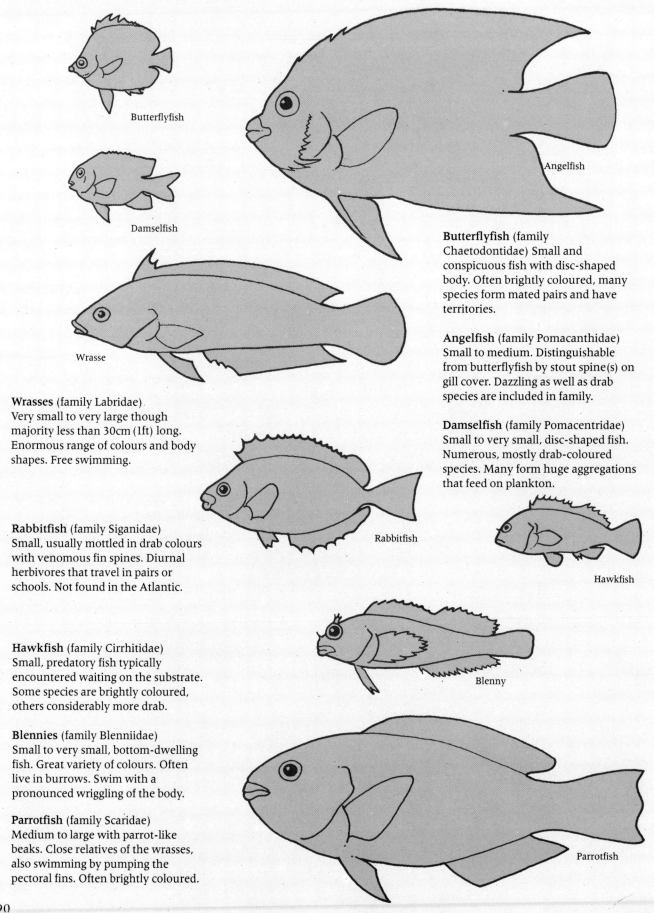

Butterflyfish

Angelfish

Damselfish

Wrasse

Rabbitfish

Hawkfish

Blenny

Parrotfish

Butterflyfish (family Chaetodontidae) Small and conspicuous fish with disc-shaped body. Often brightly coloured, many species form mated pairs and have territories.

Angelfish (family Pomacanthidae) Small to medium. Distinguishable from butterflyfish by stout spine(s) on gill cover. Dazzling as well as drab species are included in family.

Damselfish (family Pomacentridae) Small to very small, disc-shaped fish. Numerous, mostly drab-coloured species. Many form huge aggregations that feed on plankton.

Wrasses (family Labridae) Very small to very large though majority less than 30cm (1ft) long. Enormous range of colours and body shapes. Free swimming.

Rabbitfish (family Siganidae) Small, usually mottled in drab colours with venomous fin spines. Diurnal herbivores that travel in pairs or schools. Not found in the Atlantic.

Hawkfish (family Cirrhitidae) Small, predatory fish typically encountered waiting on the substrate. Some species are brightly coloured, others considerably more drab.

Blennies (family Blenniidae) Small to very small, bottom-dwelling fish. Great variety of colours. Often live in burrows. Swim with a pronounced wriggling of the body.

Parrotfish (family Scaridae) Medium to large with parrot-like beaks. Close relatives of the wrasses, also swimming by pumping the pectoral fins. Often brightly coloured.

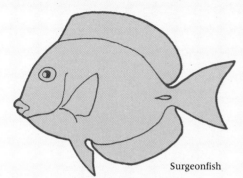

Filefish

Scorpionfish

Goby

Surgeonfish

Surgeonfish (family Acanthuridae)
Small to medium-sized fish that come
in a wide variety of colours and have
sharp spines at the base of the tail.

Filefish (family Monacanthidae)
Mostly small to medium in size. Slow
swimmers with flattened bodies and a
stout, erectable first dorsal spine.

Scorpionfish (family Scorpaenidae)
Small to medium with venomous
spines. Most are camouflaged.
Pterois and *Dendrochirus* genera more
conspicuous.

Grouper

Gobies (family Gobiidae)
Vast family of small to very small,
bottom-dwelling fish. Many are
drably coloured, others more vivid.

Triggerfish

Boxfish

Triggerfish (family Balistidae)
Medium to large with flattened
bodies and powerful mouth
bearing strong teeth. Erectable
first dorsal spine.

Porcupinefish (family Diodontidae)
Small, sluggish fish covered in stout
spines.

Porcupinefish

Groupers (family Serranidae)
Small to very large. All are carnivores
feeding on invertebrates and/or fish.
Great range of colours though many
are drably camouflaged.

Boxfish (family Ostraciidae)
Small and sluggish fish with body
enclosed by a rigid, protective casing.
Cowfish have a horn projecting from
the front of each eye.

Pufferfish (family Tetraodontidae)
Very small to medium-sized, bulbous
fish with tough, protective skin. Like
their cousins the porcupinefish, they
will swell up for protection.

Pufferfish

191

GLOSSARY

Ahermatypic Non-reef-building corals, including some hard and all soft corals, that lack symbiotic algae.

Algae Primitive plants found virtually world-wide. Some 25,000 species are known, classified according to their pigments.

Algal reef Reef formed by coralline algae.

Arborescent Term used to describe tree-like coral colonies.

Atoll reef Coral reef of circular or oval shape with a central lagoon.

Bank reef Caribbean reef separated from the shore by a lagoon.

Barbels Pair of long sensory appendages that protrudes from the chin of various fish.

Barrier reef Indo-Pacific coral reef that parallels the shore but is separated from it by a large lagoon.

Bleaching Death of coral caused by the loss of its zooxanthellae.

Bony fish Fish with bony skeleton; the vast majority of fish.

Cartilaginous fish Fish with skeletal structure predominantly composed of cartilage: the sharks, rays and chimaeras.

Class Major subdivision within a phylum.

Cnidaria Phylum that includes corals, jellyfish and anemones.

Coelenterata Alternative name for Cnidaria.

Commensalism Relatively long-term relationship between two species where one benefits and the other is unharmed.

Coralline algae A variety of red seaweed that encrusts itself with lime; immensely important to the structural health of a reef as it cements dead coral rock.

Corallite Limestone cup secreted by coral polyp.

Crustaceans Usually aquatic creatures, including crabs and lobsters, that have hard shells.

Dinoflagellates Single-celled aquatic organisms that have two different types of flagellae.

Diurnal Term used to describe creatures that become active during the day.

Encrusting Term used to describe a coral colony that grows over the substrate.

Family A group of closely related genera.

Flagellae Hair-like processes belonging to dinoflagellates, among other creatures.

Fringing reef Coral reef occurring close to and following the contours of the shore; it does not have a lagoon.

Gametes Sex cells.

Genus A group of closely related species.

Gonad Organ responsible for sex cell formation; testes of the male, ovaries of the female.

Gorgonian Soft coral whose skeleton is composed of gorgonin; includes sea fans and various sea whips.

Greenhouse effect Rise in the Earth's surface temperature due to concentrations of greenhouse gases in the atmosphere.

Greenhouse gases Gases found in the Earth's atmosphere, such as carbon dioxide, methane, water vapour and nitrous oxide, which absorb and trap long-wave radiation from the sun reflected off the Earth's surface.

Hermatypic Corals that build reefs and possess symbiotic algae.

Hybrid Offspring of two animals or plants of different species.

Invertebrate Animal lacking a backbone.

Lagoon Area of shallow water separated from the sea by a barrier, such as a reef.

Medusa form Typical body shape of jellyfish: body is shaped like a bell; the mouth is encircled by tentacles extruding from within the bell.

Mesenterial filament Thin, tentacular outgrowth of the tissue lining and sub-dividing the stomach cavity of a coral polyp. Contains both digestive juices and stinging cells and is used to attack a rival coral colony.

Mutualism Relatively long-term relationship between two different species where both partners benefit.

Nocturnal Creatures that become active during the night.

Order A group of closely related families.

Parasitism Relatively long-term relationship between two different species where one benefits and the other is harmed.

Patch reef Reef established upon irregularities of the sea floor, existing independently of a major reef formation.

Photosynthesis Process in which sunlight is used by plants to convert carbon dioxide and water into various sugars and oxygen.

Phylum Major division within animal kingdom; comprises organisms with a fundamentally similar plan, probably derived from a common ancestor.

Phytoplankton Tiny aquatic plants of very limited or no motile ability adrift in ocean currents.

Plankton Tiny aquatic creatures of very limited or no motile ability adrift in ocean currents. (*See* **Phytoplankton** *and* **Zooplankton.**)

Planula Larval stage of cnidarian drifting in open sea.

Polyp Individual, attached cnidarian with tubular body shape crested with tentacles.

Protandry Process whereby a creature actually changes sex, first producing male and then female gametes.

Protogyny Process whereby a creature actually changes sex, producing first female and then male gametes.

Reef flat Shallow area of dead coral and sand between a fringing reef and the shore.

Scleractinia The order of modern stony corals.

Species Term for individuals that can interbreed to produce fertile offspring.

Substrate or Substratum Foundation; underlying layer of material, such as rock.

Symbiosis Relatively long-term relationship between two different species. (*See* **Mutualism, Parasitism** *and* **Commensalism.**)

Vertebrate Animal with a backbone.

Zooplankton Tiny aquatic animals of very limited or no motile ability adrift in ocean currents.

Zooxanthellae Symbiotic algae found within the tissues of various animals including the scleractinian corals.

FURTHER READING

& USEFUL

ADDRESSES

Allen, Dr. Gerald R. *The Anemonefishes*, 2nd edn, Hong Kong, T. F. H. Publications, 1975

Barnes, R. S. K. and Hughes, R. N. *An Introduction to Marine Ecology*, Oxford, Blackwell, 1988

Bemert, Gunnar and Ormond, Rupert. *Red Sea Coral Reefs*, London, Kegan Paul International, 1981

Böhlke, James E. and Chaplin, Charles C. G. *Fishes of the Bahamas*, Philadelphia, Livingstone & Academy of Natural Sciences, 1970

Bunkley-Williams, Lucy and Williams, Ernest H. Jr. *Global Assault on Coral Reefs*. In *Natural History*, New York, April 1990

Caldwell, Roy. *Shrimp Surprise*. In *BBC Wildlife Magazine*, vol. 3, no. 9, pp. 415-20, Bristol and London, BBC Publications & Wildlife Publications Ltd, September 1985

Carcasson, R. H. *A Field Guide to the Coral Reef Fishes of the Indian and Western Pacific Oceans*, London, Collins, 1977

Coleman, Neville. *Australian Sea Fishes North of 30 Degrees South*, Sydney, Doubleday, 1981

Compagno, Leonard J. V. *FAO Species Catalogue*, vol. 4, parts 1 and 2 *Sharks of the World*, Rome, Food and Agriculture Organisation, 1984

Couper, Alastair (ed.). *The Times Atlas and Encyclopaedia of The Sea*, London, Times Books, 1989

Cousteau, Jacques-Yves. *Life and Death in a Coral Sea*, London, Cassell, 1971

Debelius, Helmut. *Armoured Knights of the Sea*, Frankfurt, Kernen Verlag, 1984

Duronslet, Marcel J. *et al. Kemp's Ridley Head Start and Sea Turtle Research at the Galveston Laboratory: Annual Report-Fiscal Year 1988*, National Oceanic and Atmospheric Administration Technical Memorandum NMFS-SEFC-223, May 1989

Goldsmith, Edward; Hildyard, Nicholas; McCully, Patrick and Bunyard, Peter. *5000 Days to Save The Planet*, London, Hamlyn, 1990

Grant, E. M. *Guide to Fishes*, Brisbane, The Department of Harbours and Marine, 1982

Greenberg, Idaz. *Guide to Corals and Fishes of Florida, the Bahamas and the Caribbean*, Miami, Seahawk Press, 1977

Haywood, Martyn and Wells, Sue. *The Manual of Marine Invertebrates*, London, Salamander, 1989

Hogg, Andrew. *On Film – Japan's Galapagos Slaughter*. In *The Sunday Times*, London, 9 July 1989

Humann, Paul. *Reef Fish Identification: Florida Caribbean Bahamas*, Jacksonville Florida, New World Publications, 1989

Kaplan, E. H. *A Field Guide to Coral Reefs: Caribbean and Florida*, Boston, Houghton Mifflin Company, 1982

Larson, Helen K. *A Revision of the Gobiid Genus* Bryaninops *(Pisces), with a description of six new species*. In *The Beagle, Occasional Papers of the Northern Territory Museum of Arts and Sciences*, vol. 2, no. 1, pp. 57-93, Darwin, 1985

Lowe-McConnell, R. H. *Ecological Studies in Tropical Fish Communities*, Cambridge, Cambridge University Press, 1987

Marshall, A. J. and Williams, W. D. (eds.). *Textbook of Zoology Invertebrates*, 7th edn, London, Macmillan, 1975

Maudsley, Brian. *Defenders of the Reef*. In *New Scientist*, vol. 126, no. 1714, London, New Science Publications, 28 April 1990

Miller, David and Veron, Charlie. *Biochemistry of a Special Relationship*. In *New Scientist*, vol. 126, no. 1719, pp. 44-9, London, New Science Publications, 2 June 1990

Palmer, Richard. *Coral Reefs Die for Profit*. In *The Sunday Times*, London, 25 June 1989

Randall, Dr. John E. *Red Sea Reef Fishes*, London, Immel, 1983

Randall, Dr. John E. *Sharks of Arabia*, London, Immel, 1986

Reader's Digest, Great Barrier Reef. Sydney, Reader's Digest Services Pty Ltd, 1984

Schoon, Nicholas. *Defenders of a Coral Kingdom*. In the *Independent*, London, 5 September 1989

Shapiro, Douglas Y. *Sex Reversal and Sociodemographic Processes in Coral Reef Fishes*. In *Fish Reproduction*, pp. 103-18, London, Academic Press, 1984

Smith, Margaret M. and Heemstra, Phillip C. (eds.). *Smith's Sea Fishes*, London, Springer-Verlag, 1986

Stafford-Deitsch, Jeremy. *Shark: A Photographer's Story*, London, Headline, 1987 and San Francisco, Sierra Club Books, 1987

Tait, R. V. *Elements of Marine Ecology*, 3rd edn, London, Butterworth, 1983

Thresher, Dr. R. E. *Reproduction in Reef Fishes*, Hong Kong, T. F. H. Publications, 1984

Veron, J. E. N. *Corals of Australia and the Indo-Pacific*, London, Angus & Robertson, 1986

Vine, Dr. Peter. *Red Sea Invertebrates*, London, Immel, 1986

Ward, Fred. *Florida's Coral Reefs are Imperiled*, In *National Geographic*, vol. 178, no. 1, Washington, National Geographic Society, July 1990

Ward, Peter D. *The Natural History of Nautilus*, Boston, Allen & Unwin, 1987

Watson, Lyall. *Whales of the World*, London, Hutchinson, 1985

Wells, Sue and Wood, Elizabeth. *Trading Away the Coral Reefs*. In *Oryx*, vol. 23, no. 3, pp. 121-2, Brighton, Fauna & Flora Preservation Society, July 1989

Wells, Susan M. (ed.). *Coral Reefs of the World*, 3 vols., Cambridge, United Nations Environment Programme/International Union for Conservation of Nature and Natural Resources, 1988

Wheeler, Alwyne. *The World Encyclopedia of Fishes*, London, Macdonald, 1985

Wilmoth, James H. *Biology of Invertebrata*, New Jersey, Prentice-Hall, 1967

Young, J. Z. *The Life of Vertebrates*, 2nd edn, Oxford, Oxford University Press, 1962

Zeiller, Warren. *Tropical Marine Invertebrates of Southern Florida and the Bahama Islands*, New York, John Wiley & Sons, 1974

The organizations listed below are directly involved in the conservation of coral reefs and associated flora and fauna.

UK:

The Gaia Quest Trust,
c/o Laytons,
16 Lincolns Inn Fields,
London WC2.
The Gaia Quest is involved in building a vessel that will operate in the Indian Ocean and provide a base for scientists to obtain the vital raw data on which successful conservation schemes depend. Areas for research include the shallow water communities, such as coral reefs and mangrove swamps, as well as the monitoring of sea bird, marine turtle and marine mammal populations.

Marine Conservation Society,
9 Gloucester Road,
Ross-on-Wye,
Herefordshire HR9 5BU.
The Marine Conservation Society is active in raising public awareness to the plight of coral reefs through lectures, leaflets, exhibitions and campaigns against the trade in coral reef artefacts; it is also involved in reef research world-wide.

WWF
(World Wide Fund for Nature),
Panda House,
Weyside Park,
Godalming,
Surrey GU7 1XR.
The WWF has recently launched a massive and timely campaign for the protection of the world's endangered reefs. Schemes include the establishment of marine reserves, increased research and active education of the public.

USA:

Center for Marine Conservation,
1725 DeSales St, NW,
Washington D.C. 20036.
Among its many activities, the Center for Marine Conservation is concerned with the establishment of a permanent marine sanctuary for the entire Florida Keys reef system.

Bimini Biological Field Station,
Rosenstiel School of Marine and Atmospheric Science,
Division of Marine Biology & Fisheries,
4600 Rickenbacker Causeway,
Miami, Florida 33149-1098.
The shark populations of Florida have been decimated due to unregulated over-fishing. Research into sharks in the region has therefore been forced further afield. BBFS has focused attention on the sharks of the Bahamas, offering a unique opportunity for paying members of the public to study Bahamian sharks firsthand. The finances generated by this scheme fund the vital research carried out by BBFS. The organization campaigns for the full protection of shark populations off the eastern coast of the USA, both in state waters near the coast, and federal waters further out to sea.

H.E.A.R.T. of P.W.W.S. (Help Endangered Animals Ridley Turtles of Piney Woods Wildlife Society),
P.O. Box 681231,
Houston,
Texas 77268-1231.
The Kemp's Ridley is the most endangered of all sea turtles. This volunteer group accepts donations that go towards the costs of rearing turtle hatchlings raised at Galveston Marine Laboratory.

WWF,
1250 24th St NW,
Washington D.C. 20037.
See **WWF (UK).**

Australia:
WWF,
Level 10,
8-12 Bridge St,
Sydney,
NSW 2000.
See **WWF (UK).**

New Zealand:
WWF,
35 Taranaki St,
P.O. Box 6237,
Wellington.
See **WWF (UK).**

INDEX

ACKNOWLEDGEMENTS

Editor Michele Doyle
Art Director Elaine Partington
Design Assistant Sarah Howerd
Indexer Michael Allaby
Proofreader Jocelyn Selson
Creative Director Nick Eddison
Editorial Director Ian Jackson
Production Claire Kane
and Charles James

ARTISTS
Hardlines pp 16, 25, 30, 62, 63
Sean Milne pp 22, 23, 188, 189, 190, 191

A book of this kind requires the help of many people: the ever-cheerful and indefatigable crews of boats who constantly supplied me with fully-charged scuba tanks; the researchers in various parts of the globe who effortlessly and promptly identified the most obscure creatures in my slides; and the security staff at airports who, after varying amounts of pleading, allowed my film to be hand-searched rather than X-rayed. I would especially like to thank the following: Bob and Dinah Halstead and the crew of *Telita*, Barry Hutchins, Jack and Babs Jackson, Helen Larson, Abdul Nebi and the crew of *Felicidad*, John E. Randall, Billy and Jérome Trovati, Elizabeth Wood, Alby Ziebell and the crew of *Coralita*, as well as everyone at Stella Maris in the Bahamas and Walindi Plantation in Papua New Guinea.

JEREMY STAFFORD-DEITSCH